Emotions in Sport Coaching

Emotions are widely acknowledged as an inextricable feature of human behaviour, experience and interaction. They are, arguably, the glue that can bind people together or, alternatively, drive them apart. While social scientists have paid increasing attention to the centrality of emotions in social and pedagogical relationships, the sport coaching literature has remained largely free of emotions. Indeed, there remains a paucity of scholarship exploring how emotions such as excitement, joy, anger, anxiety, guilt, pride and embarrassment may be (re-)produced in, as well as through, the social interactions and contextual relations that constitute coaching. Similarly, we know very little about how these, and other, emotions are embodied in the everyday practice of individuals and groups. The aim of this book was to generate new and exploratory insights into the emotions that are an inherent feature of social relations and individual experience in coaching. Using a variety of psychological and sociological frameworks, the chapters in this book not only explore the interconnections between emotion, identity, cognition and learning, but they also serve as a platform for stimulating further inquiry in this topic area.

The chapters were originally published in a special issue of *Sports Coaching Review.*

Paul Potrac is a Professor of Sports Coaching at Northumbria University and a Full Visiting Professor at University College Dublin. His research interests focus on the social dimensions of sport coaching and coach education, with a particular emphasis on the (micro)political and emotional features of practice.

Andy Smith is Professor of Sport and Physical Activity at Edge Hill University, Ormskirk, UK. His research interests focus on the sociology of sport, physical activity and health, with particular reference to mental health and illness.

Lee Nelson is a Reader of Sports Coaching at Edge Hill University, Ormskirk, UK. His research interests focus on the pedagogical, political and emotional features of practice in coaching and coach education contexts.

Emotions in Sport Coaching

Edited by
Paul Potrac, Andy Smith and Lee Nelson

Routledge
Taylor & Francis Group
LONDON AND NEW YORK

First published 2018 by Routledge

2 Park Square, Milton Park, Abingdon, Oxfordshire OX14 4RN
52 Vanderbilt Avenue, New York, NY 10017

Routledge is an imprint of the Taylor & Francis Group, an informa business

First issued in paperback 2020

British Library Cataloguing-in-Publication Data
A catalogue record for this book is available from the British Library

ISBN13: 978-1-138-49487-9 (hbk)
ISBN13: 978-0-367-53558-2 (pbk)

Typeset in Minion Pro
by codeMantra

Publisher's Note
The publisher accepts responsibility for any inconsistencies that may have arisen during the conversion of this book from journal articles to book chapters, namely the possible inclusion of journal terminology.

Disclaimer
Every effort has been made to contact copyright holders for their permission to reprint material in this book. The publishers would be grateful to hear from any copyright holder who is not here acknowledged and will undertake to rectify any errors or omissions in future editions of this book.

Contents

Citation Information

The chapters in this book were originally published in *Sports Coaching Review*, volume 6, issue 2 (October 2017). When citing this material, please use the original page numbering for each article, as follows:

Introduction

Emotions in sport coaching: an introductory essay
Paul Potrac, Andy Smith and Lee Nelson
Sports Coaching Review, volume 6, issue 2 (October 2017) pp. 129–141

Chapter 1

Passion and paranoia: an embodied tale of emotion, identity, and pathos in sports coaching
Paul Potrac, Cliff Mallett, Kenny Greenough and Lee Nelson
Sports Coaching Review, volume 6, issue 2 (October 2017) pp. 142–161

Chapter 2

Sport coaches' experiences of athlete injury: the development and regulation of guilt
Laura Ann Martinelli, Melissa Catherine Day and Ruth Lowry
Sports Coaching Review, volume 6, issue 2 (October 2017) pp. 162–178

Chapter 3

Understanding coach burnout and underlying emotions: a narrative approach
Kylie McNeill, Natalie Durand-Bush and Pierre-Nicolas Lemyre
Sports Coaching Review, volume 6, issue 2 (October 2017) pp. 179–196

Chapter 4

My eyes got a bit watery there: *using stories to explore emotions in coaching research and practice for injured, sick and wounded military personnel*
Kitrina Douglas and David Carless
Sports Coaching Review, volume 6, issue 2 (October 2017) pp. 197–215

Chapter 5

Emotions, identity, and power in video-based feedback sessions: tales from women's professional football
Simone Magill, Lee Nelson, Robyn Jones and Paul Potrac
Sports Coaching Review, volume 6, issue 2 (October 2017) pp. 216–232

For any permission-related enquiries please visit:
http://www.tandfonline.com/page/help/permissions

Notes on Contributors

David Carless is Professor in Narrative Psychology in the Research Institute for Sport, Physical Activity and Leisure, Leeds Beckett University, UK. David teaches qualitative research methods and gives research-informed lectures on a number of postgraduate modules. He supervises doctoral and masters students working on diverse projects such as psychosocial rehabilitation of injured military personnel, anabolic steroid use in sport, and physical activity promotion in mental health settings.

Melissa Catherine Day is a Reader in Qualitative Sport Psychology at the University of Chichester, UK. She is BASES accredited and HCPC registered and teaches at undergraduate and postgraduate level and supervises PhD students. Her areas of interest include stress, appraisal and coping, injury, trauma and disability, and the use of qualitative methods. She regularly reviews for a range of journals and is on the editorial board of *Qualitative Research in Sport, Exercise and Health.*

Kitrina Douglas is a Senior Research Fellow in the Research Institute for Sport, Physical Activity and Leisure, Leeds Beckett University, UK. She is an ambassador for the National Co-ordinating Centre for Public Engagement (NCCPE), a member of the National Anti-doping Panel for sport and a Visiting Fellow at the University of Bristol. She has an ongoing research interest in many of the problematic areas associated with performing at the top level in sports. These include: taboo issues, identity foreclosure and mental health problems.

Natalie Durand-Bush is an Associate Professor of Sport Psychology in the School of Human Kinetics at the University of Ottawa, Canada. Her research aims to understand the self-regulatory processes and skills underlying the development of optimal performance and well-being in different contexts including sport, medicine, the performing arts and academia. Dr. Durand-Bush is the co-author of the Ottawa Mental Skills Assessment Tool (OMSAT-3*©). She has also published 24 peer-reviewed articles, 4 book chapters, as well as her own lifeskills workbook. Aside from teaching and conducting research, Dr. Durand-Bush has been working for the past 17 years as a mental performance consultant with hundreds of athletes aged between 8 and 60 years and competing at different levels in various sports.

Kenny Greenough joined the Department of Sport and Physical Activity at Edge Hill University, UK, in 2008. Kenny has experience both coaching and playing at a variety of levels: professional, semi-professional, university and collegiate standard working with football players within the specific ages 16–21 years. Kenny also educated youth players within the Professional Football League. He is also a Coach Educator with the English FA.

Robyn Jones is Professor of Sport and Social Theory at the Cardiff School of Sport and Health Sciences, Cardiff Metropolitan University, and a Visiting Professor at the University College of South East Norway, Bø, Norway. His research area comprises a critical sociology of sports coaching in respect of examining the complexity of the inter-active coaching context and how practitioners manage the power-ridden dilemmas that arise. He is the General Editor of the Taylor & Francis journal *Sports Coaching Review* and also serves on the editorial boards of *Sport, Education and Society, Theories & Applications: The International Edition* and the *European Journal of Human Movement*. He is a Fellow of both the Academy of Social Sciences and the Higher Education Academy.

Pierre-Nicolas Lemyre is Associate Professor in the Department of Coaching and Psychology at the Norwegian School of Sport Sciences. His research focuses on motivational processes in elite athletes and how they are differentially related to adaptive and maladaptive sport participation outcomes. Lemyre also holds a position within the sport psychology department at the Norwegian Olympic Training Centre, and he is currently working with the national teams in swimming and biathlon while also heading a task force on the prevention of underperformance syndrome (UPS) in elite athletes. He is currently associate editor of the *International Journal of Sport Psychology*.

Ruth Lowry is a Reader in the Psychology of Active Living at the University of Chichester, UK. She is a Health and Care Professions Council–registered Practitioner Psychologist, Chartered Sport and Exercise Psychologist with the British Psychological Society, and Fellow of the Higher Education Academy. Her research interests address how physical activity can be used and measured to promote the health and wellbeing of a number of specialist populations. Ruth is chair of the BPS Division of Sport and Exercise Psychology's Training Committee. She regularly reviews for a number of journals and grant awarding bodies.

Simone Magill is a footballer for Northern Ireland and Everton Ladies FC. She has an MRes Coach Education from Edge Hill University, Ormskirk, UK.

Kylie McNeill is a doctoral candidate in the School of Human Kinetics at the University of Ottawa, Canada.

Cliff Mallett joined the School of Human Movement Studies in 2000 after a career in physical education and also in elite coaching as a National High Performance Coach in track and field with the Australian Institute of Sport (AIS) and the Queensland Academy of Sport (QAS). He teaches undergraduate and graduate students and actively researches in the area of elite sport. Prof. Mallett regularly consults with elite coaches and athletes as well as coach developers in several national sporting organisations and international organisations.

Laura Ann Martinelli is a Lecturer in Sport & Exercise Psychology at Kingston University, London. She teaches qualitative research methods as well as sport and exercise psychology. Her primary research interest is vicarious trauma in sport, with a particular focus on the impact that witnessing injury can have upon coaches.

Lee Nelson is a Reader of Sports Coaching at Edge Hill University, Ormskirk, UK. His research interests focus on the pedagogical, political and emotional features of practice in coaching and coach education contexts.

Paul Potrac is a Professor of Sports Coaching at Northumbria University and a Full Visiting Professor at University College Dublin. His research interests focus on the social dimensions of sport coaching and coach education, with a particular emphasis on the (micro) political and emotional features of practice.

Andy Smith is Professor of Sport and Physical Activity at Edge Hill University, Ormskirk, UK. His research interests focus on the sociology of sport, physical activity and health, with particular reference to mental health and illness.

Emotions in sport coaching: an introductory essay

Paul Potrac, Andy Smith and Lee Nelson

Introduction

According to Turner and Stets (2007), emotions are an inextricable feature of human experience, behaviour, and interaction. Emotions are, for them, the glue that can bind people together and, equally, drive them apart. Unfortunately, while scholars in other fields (e.g. sociology, education, and psychology) have recognised the indisputable centrality of emotions at the "micro, macro, personal, organisational, political, economic, cultural, and religious" (Denzin, 1984, p. xiii) levels of social life, the study of emotion as a central aspect of social relationships is a largely neglected feature of the sport coaching literature. Indeed, despite some notable exceptions (e.g. Jones, 2006; Nelson, Potrac, Gilbourne, Allanson, Gale, and Marshall 2013), an explicit consideration of emotion remains notably absent in the sport coaching literature, including recent attempts to develop the discipline's conceptual vocabulary (e.g. Jones, Edwards, & Viotto Filho, 2016; Lyle & Cushion, 2017; North, 2017).

Thus far, much coaching inquiry has been dominated, either overtly or implicitly, by a cognitive perspective. One of the unintended consequences of examining coaching (and indeed coach education) in this way has been the representation of coaches, coach educators, and various other contextual stakeholders (e.g. athletes, support staff, administrators) as largely rational, calculating, and dispassionate individuals who are somehow free from the constraints generated by their relations with others (Potrac, Jones, Purdy, Nelson, & Marshall, 2013). In this respect, sport coaching researchers have rarely examined how emotions such as excitement, joy, anger, anxiety, guilt and embarrassment are (re-)produced in, as well as through, the social relationships and interactions that constitute coaching and coach education practice (Jones, Potrac, Cushion, & Ronglan, 2011; Potrac, Jones, Gilbourne,

& Nelson, 2013; Potrac, Jones, Purdy et al. 2013). Similarly, our understanding of coaches' decision-making has also yet to examine how emotions play an integral role in helping individuals and groups of coaches to narrow down "the range of potential actions into a manageable assortment" (Potrac et al., 2013, p. 238) on which they can draw in their everyday practice. In addition, a greater appreciation of emotions as "a permanent dimension of our being in the world and being towards others" (Crossley, 2011, p. 62) in our relational networks would enhance our understandings and representations of the "coalitions, conflicts, and negotiations" (Fineman, 2005, p. 2) that characterise the activity of coaching (Jones et al., 2011; Potrac & Jones, 2009a, 2009b; Thompson, Potrac, & Jones, 2015). Equally, as a community of scholars, we are yet to consider the ways in which routine, but immensely powerful, emotions such as hope, anger, pride, anxiety, and boredom are "frequent, pervasive, manifold, and often intense" (Pekrun & Linnenbrink-Garcia, 2014, p. 1) features of coach and athlete learning.

The paucity of research addressing emotion in sport coaching likely owes much to the relatively short history of coaching scholarship and the hitherto dominance of highly individualised and rationalised conceptions of coaching, rather than any conscious effort by scholars and educators to purposefully relegate emotion to the "ontological basement" of inquiry (Liston & Garrison, 2003, p. 5). For us, the study of emotion can help us build upon the significant intellectual developments that have characterised this fledgling field of inquiry (Lyle & Cushion, 2017). Specifically, such inquiry can complement the largely cognitive-oriented perspectives of social action in coaching by focusing on the structuring and generation of emotion within the complex networks of relationships of which coaches (and others) are a part (see Potrac & Marshall, 2011; Potrac et al., 2013).

It is against this backdrop that we chose to pursue this special issue on the emotional dimensions of sport coaching. Our motivations for this project were various and interconnected. On one level, inspiration came from some of our own embodied, emotional, experiences as coaches, coach educators and sports participants. While they often varied in duration, intensity and connection, emotions such as joy, pride, guilt, and anger have been (and remain) constant companions in our respective coaching and sporting "careers" (e.g. Potrac et al., 2013). For us, emotions are not something that can be turned on and off so that we are sometimes emotional and at other times not (Crossley, 2011). Instead, our respective experiences always maintain an affective dimension. What varies, however, is the flavour and the intensity of affect (Crossley, 2011). Equally, our emotions are never absent from our relationships with, and connections to, other people in our respective coaching worlds; be it in the past, present, or, indeed, projected future (Crossley, 2011; Denzin, 1984). Indeed, our coaching practices have been variously "shaped, negotiated, rejected, reformed, fought over, [and] celebrated because of feelings" (Fineman, 2005, p. 1); both ours and those of others. In this regard, we concluded that our experiences in the field certainly did not, and do not, match with the accounts of practice that we frequently read about in, and had contributed to, the body of knowledge in sport coaching.

We also found, and continue to find, this state of affairs to be problematic when helping students to consider realistically the demands that coaching can make of people (Harris, 2015). For us, coaching is not about unproblematic recipes and "guaranteed" prescriptions, or, indeed, heroic individual performances (Jones et al., 2011). Instead, the essence of coaching lies in how we manage "the pressures, constraints, and possibilities of context" (Jones et al., 2011, p. 4). Here, we frequently wished for a rich, developed, and subject specific body of literature upon which to illustrate and consider how the ambiguities, pathos, and everyday politics of coaching are felt by individuals and groups, be they coaches, athletes, parents, or administrators (Harris, 2015; Jones et al., 2011). Over time, we grew increasingly concerned about the apparent disjuncture between the material we presented in our respective coaching courses (i.e. how we might coach) and the emotional realities (i.e. how we, and others, might think about and experience coaching) that we discussed informally with coaches, athletes, and coach educators in various sport settings.

In taking steps to address our concerns, we were thankful to be able to draw upon the contributions made by various and eminent scholars in mainstream social science (e.g. Bolton, 2005; Denzin, 1984; Fineman, 2005, 2008; Turner & Stets, 2005) and education (e.g. Day & Lee, 2011; Leithwood & Beatty, 2007; Schutz & Pekrun, 2007; Schutz & Zembylas, 2009; Zembylas, 2005). Rather than providing theoretical tinsel, as some have suggested, our engagement with such scholarship has undoubtedly advanced our own thinking, teaching, and, indeed, research in sport coaching (Potrac, Jones, & Nelson, 2014). In addition to the frameworks utilised in the papers that comprise this special issue, we have found Hargreaves's (1998) theorising on the emotional practice and politics of teaching and Thoits's (2013) consideration of emotions, social ties, and wellbeing to be particularly insightful. While we primarily make connections between these respective works and potential avenues for researching coaches' emotions below, we recognise that their application could extend to all those who comprise the social networks of coaching (e.g. athletes, performance analysts, strength and conditioners, sport psychologists, parents, and administrators) and coach education (e.g. coach learners, assessors, administrators). Equally, we do not position these frameworks as the most adequate, or only, ways for researching and understanding emotion in sport coaching. Instead, we simply believe that they provide some productive starting points for more fruitful investigations of emotions in sport coaching.

In his article addressing the emotional politics of teaching and teacher development, Hargreaves (1998) proposed several interconnected points about the emotional dimensions of teaching that coaching researchers and coach educators may wish to consider in their own research and applied endeavours. Firstly, in drawing upon the work of Denzin (1984), Hargreaves (1998, p. 320) proposed that, like all aspects of social life, our engagements in pedagogical activity are not just technical and cognitive. He argued that:

> … as an *emotional practice* [our italics], teaching activates, colours, and expresses teachers' own feelings, and the actions in which those feelings are embedded. Likewise,

> as an emotional practice, teaching activates colours and otherwise affects the feelings and actions of others with whom teachers work and form relationships. Teachers can enthuse their students or bore them; be approachable to parents or alienate them; feel supported by their colleagues (and therefore willing to take risks in improving their craft) or mistrusted by them (and therefore more inclined to play safe).

These arguments could equally be made about coaching, whether in high performance, development, or community settings (Lyle & Cushion, 2017), as the papers in this volume and elsewhere suggest (e.g. Jones, 2006; Nelson et al., 2013; Purdy & Potrac, 2016; Purdy, Potrac, & Jones, 2008; Potrac et al., 2013).

Hargreaves (1998) also noted how teaching entails *emotional understanding* and *emotional labour*. The former, refers to:

> … an intersubjective process requiring a person to enter into the field of experience of another and experience for himself or herself the same or similar experiences experienced by another. The subjective interpretation of another's emotional experience from one's own standpoint is central to emotional understanding. Shared and shareable emotionality lie at the core of what it means to understand and meaningfully enter into the emotional experiences of another. (Denzin, 1984, p. 137)

In the context of coaching, emotional understanding refers to a coach seeking to comprehend the intentions, thoughts, feelings, and behaviours of others using empathy and emotional imagination (Hargreaves, 1998). Given the importance of obtaining, maintaining, and advancing a connection with athletes (and other situational stakeholders), examining how coaches recognise and respond to fear, pride, embarrassment, and disgust in others is a potentially fruitful avenue of inquiry for advancing our understanding of coaches' pedagogical and micro-political tact (Hargreaves, 1998).

In drawing upon the classic work of Hochschild (1983), Hargreaves (1998) argued that teaching entails active emotional labour. Here, emotional labour refers to work that:

> … requires one to induce or suppress feelings in order to sustain the outward countenance that produces the proper state of mind in others … This kind of labour calls for co-ordination of mind and feeling, and it sometimes draws on a source of self that we honour as deep and integral to our personality. (Hochschild, 1983, p. 322)

For Hargreaves (1998), the emotional labour of teaching entails more than superficially acting out feeling such as surprise or disappointment. For example, he also suggested that it requires "consciously working one-self up into a state of actually experiencing the necessary feelings that are required to perform one's job well" (Hargreaves, 1998, p. 322). Hargreaves (1998) further argued that emotional labour is not always a negative phenomenon where individuals feel obliged to trade parts of their self for the security and rewards they obtain from employers. Instead, he contended that there are positive aspects to emotional labour, including circumstances where an individual understands his or her emotional performances to be a genuine form of giving to others (such as enhancing their learning). Emotional labour is, however, also something that can be turned against the person exercising it, be it through increasing performance expectations and workload, stress, and extreme self-sacrifice that have potentially profound consequences for burnout and teacher cynicism (Hargreaves, 1998). While the concept of emotional labour and emotion management has received some initial attention in the coaching literature (e.g. Cassidy, Jones, & Potrac, 2016; Nelson et al., 2013; Potrac & Marshall, 2013), they remain a little understood and under-researched aspect of coaches' (and other stakeholders') lives.

Hargreaves (1998) further described how the emotions of teaching are also shaped by the *moral purposes* of those who teach and how workplace conditions allow them to achieve their desired goals and purposes. While the fulfilment of our moral purposes can result in happiness, joy, and pride, the failure to be able to pursue or achieve them can lead an individual to experience emotions such as guilt, anxiety, anger, and frustration. In an educational context, Hargreaves (1998) suggested that these emotions can be experienced and shaped by teachers' engagement in contexts when they: (a) face perceived obstructions (e.g. increased form-filling, meetings, and performance assessment); (b) are compelled to achieve other people's goals that they find inappropriate (e.g. mandated curricular and standardised teaching episodes); (c) are required to pursue standards that are defined too ambitiously for the learners in their charge; and (d) are unable to choose between multiple (and sometimes) conflicting goals. For Hargreaves (1998), it is a sense of loss relating to moral purposes that can lead educators to feel *demoralised*. In the context of coaching, Hargreaves's (1998) work on moral purposes helps us to consider how coaches' emotions are inextricably tied to their purposes (formal and perceived), what stakes they have and are asked to have in them, whether the conditions of the coaching setting make them achievable or not, and the implications these have for coach retention and wellbeing (Cassidy et al., 2015).

Hargreaves's (1998) theorising also acknowledges how teachers' emotions are rooted in, as well as affect, their selves, identities, and relationships with others. He suggested that many of the emotions that "we feel are intimately related to our sense of physical safety, psychological security and moral integrity" (Hargreaves, 1998, p. 323) and can vary temporally, spatially, and contextually. Feelings of security, being valued, wanted, and protected, he contends, can lead to happiness, while the opposite can result in experiences of fear, shame, and anxiety (Hargreaves, 1998). In this regard, Hargreaves (1998) argued that working with others is often an intense and emotionally laden experience. For example, collaborating with, performing for, or being judged by, others often entails some degree of discomfort and anxiety, as individuals are, for all intense purposes, putting their professional persona and sense of self "at risk" (Hargreaves, 1998).

While he recognised that risk itself is not an emotion, Hargreaves (1998) argued that it is certainly capable of generating strong emotions in context-dependent ways. These include "the fear and anxiety of confronting danger and threat, as well as the exhilaration of mastery and achievement when difficulties have been surmounted" (Hargreaves, 1998, pp. 324, 325). While a certain level of individual anxiety is essential to pedagogical risk-taking and professional development, Hargreaves (1998) suggested that it needs to be balanced with collective feelings of security, trust, and a sense of being valued. While coaching researchers have begun to explore the interconnections between a coach's sense of self, organisational relationships, and inter-personal trust (e.g. Jones, 2006; Potrac, Jones, Gilbourne et al., 2013; Purdy & Potrac, 2016; Purdy, Potrac, & Nelson, 2013), little explicit attention has been given to the inherent emotional components of these interdependencies. Equally, there has yet to be any concerted effort to explore coaches' (and other stakeholders') experiences of specific positive (e.g. happiness, joy, pride) and negative (e.g. fear, shame, anger) emotions which are grounded in an individual's sense-making and responses to the actions and behaviours of others (Burkitt, 2014).

The penultimate point addressed by Hargreaves (1998) concerns teachers' experiences and perceptions of *power* and *powerlessness*. At the heart of his argument is the recognition that "emotions are a political as well as personal phenomena" (Hargreaves, 1998, p. 326). In drawing upon the writings of Kemper (1995), Hargreaves (1998) contended that when an individual perceives and experiences themselves occupying a greater position of power, he or she may feel more secure, while increased status (whether defined formally or informally) can also lead to feelings of happiness, pride, and gratitude. No less importantly, Hargreaves (1998) claimed that when people experience a threat (real and/or perceived) to their position of power and status, this can invoke fear, anxiety, shame and depression (Hargreaves, 1998). These emotions are simultaneously affected by the micro-politics of the organisations of which individuals are a part, as well as the wider neoliberal values and policy milieu in which the activity occurs (Hargreaves, 1998). While the political nature of coaching has been the subject of some initial inquiry (e.g. Potrac & Jones, 2009a, 2009b; Potrac et al., 2013; Thompson et al., 2015, among others), there has been little consideration of the various emotions that are at the heart of these dynamics and interactions. In this context, the study of emotions may enable to us to understand better not only how coaches experience various acts of collaboration, negotiation, and conflict within their everyday lives, but also why they interpret and respond to them in the ways that they do.

The final component of Hargreaves's (1998) work is concerned with *culture* and *context*. Here, Hargreaves (1998) addressed how the emotions some individuals experience, and the decisions they take to reveal or conceal them, may "vary among cultures, occupations, genders, and ethnocultural groups" (Hargreaves, 1998, p. 329). By way of an example, he contrasted Nias (1996) disapproval of teachers' anger in British primary school classrooms with the North American Native Indian Medicine Way Path of Learning, which "values anger at injustice as something worth cultivating in students" (Hargreaves, 1998, p. 329). For Hargreaves (1998, p. 329) there is much to gain from recognising how "emotions and their legitimate expression … are culturally loaded, being afforded different value within different cultural, racial, and ethnic groups". When applied to coaching and coach education, Hargreaves's (1998) insights may help us to understand how coach recruitment and development is not an emotionally or morally neutral process. Instead, these activities include exposure to the political and cultural sensitivities and differences in the relations between the groups involved (Hargreaves, 1998), and the dynamic power differentials which characterise their relationships.

The interactionist work of Thoits (1989, 2004, 2011) also raises a number of conceptual ideas that might usefully inform future research on emotions in sport coaching scholarship. For Thoits, the investigation of everyday emotions should not be restricted to their innate, biophysical features. Instead, she argues for a greater recognition of how emotions, such as anger, fear, happiness, disgust, and sadness, are grounded in social relationships where "subjective experiences and emotional beliefs are both socially acquired and socially structured" (Thoits, 1989, p. 319). In this regard, Thoits (1989, 2004, 2011) attaches considerable importance to investigating the normative content of emotions acquired through processes of emotional socialisation not least because, for her, "emotion norms not only define situationally appropriate feelings and displays" (Thoits, 2004, p. 364), but they also inform people's sense making and responses to their social contexts. Like Hargreaves (1998), Thoits (2004) suggests that emotional expectations are context-dependent and that societies can be comprised of "multiple, overlapping and potentially conflicting emotional ideologies" (p. 365). In sport coaching, Thoits's (1989, 2004, 2011) work should encourage us to understand better how these ideologies may be deliberately produced and reproduced to justify and/or serve the preferred goals of individuals, groups, specific organisations and whole industries. Thoits's (1989, 2004, 2011) insights also raise important questions about how emotional rules are socially learnt and shape the evaluations, expressions, and practices of coaches, athletes, and other key stakeholders.

In her analysis of literature addressing workplace emotion, Thoits (2004) highlighted how employees across a range of organisations and roles have actively conformed to the emotion rules of their working contexts. According to Thoits (2004), they do so to secure the social approval of significant others, avoid those sanctions associated with the violation of these normative expectations, and, above all, to help evade the kinds of social evaluative threats which have been shown to impact negatively on health and wellbeing. Her critical review also addressed a range of emotion management strategies used by employees. These include cognitively reframing social situations to elicit alternative emotional responses, altering their physiological state through bodily work, and performing desired behaviours through purposive expression work (Thoits, 2004). In a similar vein to the work of Hargreaves (1998), Thoits's (1989, 2004, 2011) work sensitises us to how coaches' social and emotional performances relate to individual and group understandings of normative expectations, social approval, and sanctions, as well as how these contribute to the health and wellbeing of those involved.

In addition to the management of their own emotions, Thoits (1989, 2004, 2011) explores how employees influence the emotions of those with whom they work, a process she refers to as *interpersonal emotion management.* Developing an understanding of this feature of organisational life is, for her, of considerable importance to explaining why acts of "cohesion, cooperation, and loyalty" as well as "conflict, discrimination, injustice, and cruelty" may occur (Thoits, 2004, p. 369). In her discussion of the social function of emotional conformity and the responsive interpretation of others' emotions, Thoits (2004, 2011) drew upon Cahill's (1999) notion of *emotional capital.* This refer to an individual's understanding of the cultural norms and expectations of his or her social contexts, as well as their ability to regulate and transform their own and other's emotions (Thoits, 2004, 2011). She explained that those possessing considerable emotional capital have the potential to "deliberately manipulate other people's emotions to sustain, usurp, upset, or withhold social placement from some and to convey it to others (or themselves)" (Thoits, 2004, p. 371). Emotional capital also permits workers to "evaluate the self from the perspective of other people" (Thoits, 2004, p. 372) so that they may strategically conform to the expectations of others. This can feature in the restoring and repairing of self-image when damaged, and manipulating others' emotions for personal benefits or gain (Thoits, 2004). To date, there has yet to be any concerted effort to explore if coaches seek to manage the emotions of those key contextual stakeholders with whom they interact, the interactional strategies that they use to obtain desired outcomes, and the reasoning that underpins this aspect of their practice.

According to Thoits (2004, 2011), sensitivity to the emotional experiences of others permits people to actively develop a sense of collective identity and social solidarity in ways that can positively impact upon social and psychological wellbeing. She claimed that the everyday emotional (in addition to informational and instrumental) support that individuals may receive in their relationships with others not only helps to sustain their self-esteem and sense of belonging, but also the level of control that an they perceive themselves to have over future events (Thoits, 2011). In addition to routine everyday emotional support, Thoits (2011) contends that the caring, sympathetic, and comforting presence offered by significant primary and secondary group members may reduce physical and psychological adversity during times of distress. She explained that individuals, who have experienced similar stressful situations, are particularly able to offer empathic and tolerant understandings of another's concerns and emotional reactions. Such interactions, she argued, can help to validate the normalcy of the other's emotional reactions, reduce the psychological arousal that he or she may be experiencing, as well as strengthen low self-esteem (Thoits, 2011). While researchers have started to investigate how coaches' interactions with other stakeholders may impact upon people's self-esteem (e.g. Thompson et al., 2013; Potrac et al., 2013), little explicit attention has been given to examining how the actions of others may impact, positively and negatively, on coaches' psychological wellbeing (Nelson, in press). This certainly represents an important strand of inquiry, especially in terms of assisting and retaining coaches in high performance, developmental, and community settings.

For us, the work of Hargreaves (1998) and Thoits (1989, 2004, 2011) raises several important issues worthy of investigation. Firstly, there is a clear need to develop a greater understanding of coaching as an emotional practice that likely entails (considerable) emotional labour. Indeed, we know very little about how coaches manage their own emotions, as well as attempt to influence the emotional experiences of others. Secondly, while the technical competencies of coaching are important, locating coaches and their emotions within the complex networks of relationships in which they are bound-up is an important starting point for better understanding the realities of coaching practice. Doing so will also help avoid emotions being relegated to the position of "sentimental adornments" (Hargreaves, 1998, p. 330) in comparison to the technical and functional parts of a coach's (and other stakeholders') work. Thirdly, there is perhaps much to gain, both theoretically and practically, from explicitly examining the interconnections between the moral purposes of coaches, the political dynamics of coaching policy and organisational life, the social relationships that comprise coaching, and the significant personal investments made in this activity (Hargreaves, 1998; Thoits, 1989, 2004, 2011). Fourthly, they also encourage us to recognise how the emotional politics of coaching and coach education may vary from one coach to another, from one context to another, and from one society and time period to another. Finally, there is much work to be done on the emotional support that coaches do (or do not) receive in the workplace, how the interrelated features (and often blurring) of their working and private lives impacts on their health and wellbeing, and how coaches' behaviours can impact on the wellbeing of their athletes.

In practical terms, curriculum leaders and developers, including ourselves, arguably need to do more to embrace the emotional dimensions of coaching and coach development. An initial first step in this regard might be to "acknowledge and even honour the centrality of the emotions to the processes" (Hargreaves, 1998, p. 333). of coaching, learning, performance, and caring in practice. While various educational strategies could be utilised to achieve this goal (see Beatty 2004, 2006, 2007), the overarching intent should be "to put the heart back into" coaching, learning, and leading in a sincere manner and for the benefit of all (Hargreaves, 1998, p. 333).

The papers in this special issue

For this special issue, we subscribed to the definition of emotion developed by Turner and Stets (2005). They suggested that emotions consist of five core elements:

> (a) the biological activation of key body systems; (b) socially constructed definitions and constraints on what emotions should be experienced and expressed in a situation; (c) the application of linguistic labels provided by culture to internal sensations; (d) the

> over expression of emotions through facial, voice, and other paralinguistic moves; and (e) perceptions and appraisal of situational objects or events. (Turner & Stets, 2005, p. 9)

While no single element can explain when, how, and why emotions are expressed and understood in particular ways, the articles in this issue specifically focus on the socially constructed, personally enacted, and embodied features of coaches' and athletes' emotions. In doing so, we do not deny individual, physical, and psychical dimensions of emotions, but, instead, seek to understand them from a broadly social-relational perspective (Cantó-Milà, 2016).

In the first paper, "Passion and paranoia: An embodied tale of emotion, identity, and pathos in sport coaching", Potrac, Mallett, Greenough, and Nelson address the lead author's (emotional) understandings of coaching an amateur women's football team. Through a process of collaborative inquiry, the authors consider how a coach's embodied emotional experiences and meaning making were produced in, as well as through, the interaction of self and other in the club context. Following the presentation of storied experience, the complementary works of Burkitt (1997, 2014) and Scott (2015) are deployed as the primary heuristic devices. Here, the authors' interpretation focuses on the interconnections between emotion, identity, and embodied experience. In concluding the paper, Potrac et al. advocate a greater integration of emotion into ongoing and future coaching scholarship.

The next article, by Martinelli, Day and Lowry, focuses on coaches' experiences of guilt in relation to athlete injury. In-depth semi-structured interviews were used to generate data concerning coaches' understandings of the development and regulation of guilt. The coaches' stories were then critically interrogated using psychological theorising concerning trauma-related guilt. As well as illuminating how guilt may be embodied and managed in different ways by coaches, the authors also raise some important concerns regarding the deontological approach used to define a "good" coach in much coach education provision. In particular, Martinelli et al. argue that dominant discourses regarding coaches' obligations and athletes' entitlements may be instrumental in entrenching coaches' experiences of guilt in everyday practice.

The third paper by McNeill, Durand-Bush, and Lemyre investigates coaches' understandings of burnout. Based on in-depth interviews with professional coaches, the authors present five non-fictional short stories highlighting the emotions that underpinned the coaches' experiences and sense making. As well as examining emotions such as anxiety, anger, apathy, and dejection, the authors also consider these emotions in relation to the three dimensions of burnout; namely, emotional exhaustion, depersonalisation, and reduced personal accomplishment. Finally, the authors highlight the need for further intervention research that aims to better understand, reduce, and manage coach burnout.

The penultimate contribution is provided by Douglas and Carless. For this study, ethnographic data were collected at a golf intervention where civilian coaches worked among serving injured, sick, and wounded military personnel in a recovery setting. Through the utilisation of a series of vignettes, the authors consider how emotions are evoked, hidden, or made visible depending on different social situations and relationships. The stories also reveal some of the potential costs or risks of becoming more empathetic and caring. The authors conclude the paper by considering the value of narrative inquiry for illuminating the social and emotional aspects of our lives, work, and relationships that can otherwise be difficult to articulate and share.

In the final paper, Magill, Nelson, Jones, and Potrac consider the emotional dimensions of athletes' everyday participation in video-based feedback sessions. Data for this study were obtained through a process of collaborative critical reflection and in-depth interviews with elite female footballers. Using fictional narratives as their mode of representation, the authors highlight the emotional, embodied, and relational features of two athletes' experiences of video-based feedback. Burkitt's (1999, 2014) writings addressing (complex) emotions and social relations are used as the primary sense-making framework, with the analysis focusing on the interconnections between sensate, corporeal experience, and the power relations and interdependencies in which high performance athletes are enmeshed. In their conclusion, Magill et al. suggest that the exploration of individual emotion management within a network of social relations would help us to understand better the emotionality of athletes (and other stakeholders) within high performance sport settings.

Disclosure statement

No potential conflict of interest was reported by the authors.

References

Beatty, B. (2006). Becoming emotionally prepared for leadership: Courage, counter-intuition and commitment to connectedness. *International Journal of Knowledge Culture and Change, 6*, 51–66.

Beatty, B. (2007). Feeling the future of school leadership: Learning to lead with emotions in mind. *Leading and Managing, 13*, 44–65.

Beatty, B., & Brew, C. (2004). Trusting relationships and emotional epistemologies: 1a foundational leadership issue. *School Leadership and Management, 24*, 329–356.

Bolton, S. (2005). *Emotion management in the workplace*. Basingstoke: Palgrave Macmillan.

Burkitt, I. (1997). Social relationships and emotions. *Sociology, 31*, 37–55.

Burkitt, I. (1999). *Bodies of thought: Embodiment, identity and modernity*. London: Sage.

Burkitt, I. (2014). *Emotions and social relations*. London: Sage.

Cassidy, T., Jones, R., & Potrac, P. (2016). *Understanding sports coaching: The social, cultural and pedagogical foundations of coaching practice* (3rd ed.). London: Routledge.

Cantó-Milà, N. (2016). Linking emotions: Emotions as the invisible threads that bind people together. *Sociological Research Online, 21*, 10.

Crossley, N. (2011). *Towards relational sociology*. London: Routledge.

Day, C., & Lee, J. (2011). *New understandings of teacher's work*. Dordrecht: Springer.

Denzin, N. (1984). *On understanding emotion*. San Francisco, CA: Jossey-Bass.

Fineman, S. (2005). *Understanding emotion at work*. London: Sage.

Fineman, S. (2008). *The emotional organisation: Passions and power*. Oxford: Blackwell Publishing.

Hargreaves, A. (1998). The emotional politics of teaching and teacher development: With implications for educational leadership. *International Journal of Leadership in Education, 1*, 315–336.

Harris, S. (2015). *An invitation to the sociology of emotion*. London: Routledge.

Hochschild, A. (1983). *The managed heart: The commercialisation of human feeling*. Berkeley: University of California Press.

Jones, R. (2006). Dilemmas, maintaining "face" and paranoia: An average coaching life. *Qualitative Inquiry, 12*, 1012–1021.

Jones, R., Edwards, C., & Viotto Filho, I. (2016). Activity theory, complexity and sports coaching: An epistemology for a discipline. *Sport, Education and Society, 21*, 200–216.

Jones, R., Potrac, P., Cushion, C., & Ronglan, L. T. (Eds.). (2011). *The sociology of sports coaching*. London: Routledge.

Kemper, T. (1995). Sociological models in the explanation of emotions. In M. Lewis & J. Haviland (Eds.), *Handbook of Emotions* (pp. 41–51). New York, NY: The Guilford Press.

Leithwood, K., & Beatty, B. (Eds.). (2007). *Leading with teacher emotions in mind*. Thousand Oaks, CA: Corwin Press.

Liston, D., & Garrison, J. (2003). *Teaching, learning and loving : Reclaiming passion in educational practice*. New York, NY: Routledge.

Lyle, J., & Cushion, C. (2017). *Sports coaching concepts : A framework for coaching practice*. London: Routledge.

Nelson, L. (in press). The deconstruction and reconstruction of sports coaching: An interview with Professor Robyn Jones: A commentary. *International Journal of Sports Science and Coaching*.

Nelson, L., Potrac, P., Gilbourne, D., Allanson, A., Gale, L., & Marshall, P. (2013). Thinking, feeling, acting: The case of a semi-professional soccer coach. *Sociology of Sport Journal, 19*, 19–40.

Nias, J. (1996). Thinking about feeling: The emotions in teaching. *Cambridge Journal of Education, 26*, 293–306.

North, J. (2017). *Sports coaching research and practice: Ontology, interdisciplinarity and critical realism*. London: Routledge.

Pekrun, R., & Linnenbrink-Garcia, L. (2014). *International handbook of emotions in education*. London: Routledge.

Potrac, P., & Jones, R. (2009a). Micro-political workings in semi-professional football coaching. *Sociology of Sport Journal, 26*, 557–577.

Potrac, P., & Jones, R. (2009b). Power, conflict and co-operation: Towards a micro-politics of coaching. *Quest, 61*, 223–236.

Potrac, P., & Marshall, P. (2011). Arlie Russell Hochschild: The managed heart, feeling rules, and emotional labour: Coaching as an emotional endeavour. In R. Jones, P. Potrac, C. Cushion, & L. T. Ronglan (Eds.), *The sociology of sports coaching* (pp. 54–66). London: Routledge.

Potrac, P., Jones, R., Gilbourne, D., & Nelson, L. (2013). Handshakes, BBQs, and bullets: A tale of self-interest and regret in football coaching. *Sports Coaching Review, 1*, 79–92.

Potrac, P., Jones, R., & Nelson, L. (2014). Interpretivism. In L. Nelson, R. Groom, & P. Potrac (Eds.), *Research methods in sports coaching* (pp. 31–41). London: Routledge.

Potrac, P., Jones, R., Purdy, L., Nelson, J., & Marshall, P. (2013). Coaches, coaching, and emotion: A suggested research agenda. In P. Potrac, W. Gilbert, & J. Denison (Eds.), *The Routledge handbook of sports coaching* (pp. 235–246). London: Routledge.

Purdy, L., & Potrac, P. (2016). Am I just not good enough? The creation, development and questioning of a coaching identity. *Sport, Education & Society, 21*, 778–795.

Purdy, L., Potrac, P., & Jones, R. (2008). Power, consent and resistance: An autoethnography of competitive rowing. *Sport, Education, & Society, 13*, 319–336.

Purdy, L., Potrac, P., & Nelson, L. (2013). Trust, distrust and coaching practice. In P. Potrac, W. Gilbert, & J. Denison (Eds.), *The Routledge handbook of sports coaching* (pp. 309–320). London: Routledge.

Schutz, P., & Pekrun, R. (2007). *Emotion in education*. Amsterdam: Elsevier.

Schutz, P., & Zembylas, M. (2009). *Advances in teacher emotion research*. Dordrecht: Springer.

Scott, S. (2015). *Negotiating identity: Symbolic interactionist approaches to social identity.* Cambridge: Polity Press.

Thoits, P. A. (1989). The sociology of emotions. *Annual Review of Sociology, 15*, 317–342.

Thoits, P. A. (2004). Emotion norms, emotion work, and social order. In A. Manstead, N. Frijda, & A. Fischer (Eds.) *Feelings and emotions: The Amsterdam symposium* (pp. 359–378). New York, NY: Cambridge University Press.

Thoits, P. A. (2011). Mechanisms linking social ties and support to physical and mental health. *Journal of Health and Social Behavior, 52*, 145–161.

Thoits, P. A. (2013). Self, identity, stress and mental health. In C. Aneshensel, J. Phelan, & A. Bierman (Eds.) *Handbook of the sociology of the mental* (pp. 357–377). The Netherlands: Springer.

Thompson, A., Potrac, P., & Jones, R. (2015). 'I found out the hard way': Micro-political workings in professional football. *Sport, Education & Society, 20*, 976–994.

Turner, J., & Stets, J. (2005). *The sociology of emotions*. Cambridge: Cambridge University Press.

Turner, J., & Stets, J. (2007). Moral emotions. In J. Stets & J. Turner (Eds.), *Handbook of the sociology of emotion* (pp. 544–566). New York, NY: Springer.

Zembylas, M. (2005). *Teaching with emotion: A postmodern enactment.* Greenwich, CT: Information Age.

Passion and paranoia: an embodied tale of emotion, identity, and pathos in sports coaching

Paul Potrac, Cliff Mallett, Kenny Greenough and Lee Nelson

ABSTRACT
In response to the wider call to put the person back into the study of coaching, this paper addresses my, the lead author's, understandings of coaching an amateur women's football team. Specifically, my co-authors and I critically consider how my embodied emotional experiences and meaning-making were produced in, as well as through, the interaction of the self and other in the club context. Following the presentation of my storied experiences, the complementary works of Burkitt and Scott are deployed as the primary heuristic devices. Here, our interpretation focuses on the interconnections between emotion, identity, and embodied experience. Rather than seeking to provide a singular truth, however, theory is, instead, used to reveal, clarify, and make ambiguous experience more apparent to the reader. In concluding the paper, we advocate a greater integration of emotion into ongoing and future coaching scholarship.

Introduction

In response to the wider call to put the person back into the study of coaching (e.g. Jones, Potrac, Cushion, & Ronglan, 2011; Potrac, Jones, Gilbourne, & Nelson, 2013a; Potrac, Jones, Purdy, Nelson, & Marshall, 2013b), this paper addresses my, the lead author's, understandings of coaching Erewhon Town FC (a pseudonym), an amateur women's soccer team. On one level, my co-authors and I seek to provide a highly personalised and embodied tale of the excitement, joy, guilt, anxiety, and frustration that I experienced as a part of everyday life at the football club. On another level, our intention is to illustrate how these emotions were interconnected with my identity as a coach (Purdy & Potrac, 2016 Scott, 2015; Thompson, Potrac, & Jones, 2015). Here, we critically consider how my emotional experiences and sense-making were produced in, as well as through, the interaction of the self and other in a particular social context (Nelson et al., 2014; Potrac, Nelson, & O'Gorman, 2016; Scott, 2015). Rather than viewing emotions as solely "internal to an individual and his or her biological constitution" (Burkitt, 1997; p. 127), we hope to illustrate how they might be generated, experienced, and expressed through an individual's interdependent relations with others (Burkitt, 1997, 2014).

The significance of this paper lies in the breaking of new ground in the theorisation of coaching as a problematic, emotional, and ethical activity (Jones, 2009; Potrac et al., 2013b). Despite calls to recognise emotion in sports coaching, there remains, aside from some notable exceptions (e.g. Jones, 2006; Nelson et al., 2014; Potrac & Marshall, 2011), a paucity of literature addressing how emotions such as guilt, joy, anxiety, frustration, and anger are enacted, embodied, and produced in social relations with others (Jones et al., 2011; Potrac et al., 2013b). In many ways, this state of affairs could be understood to reflect the scale and maturity of coaching scholarship. However, we believe the failure to meaningfully engage with emotions, as well as their interconnections with "cognition, self, context, ethical judgement and purposeful action" (Kelchtermans, 2005, p. 996), leaves the field open to the accusation of producing strangely inhuman and asocial accounts of practice (Burkitt, 2014; Jones, Armour, & Potrac, 2004; Jones, Edwards, & Viotto Filho, 2016; Potrac et al., 2013a, 2013b). From our perspective, consideration of these issues can also contribute to a better understanding of what it means to be a coach, including the intersections between professional and private selves. Relatedly, such inquiry could be used to support coaches' professional development, personal wellbeing, and continued engagement in this role (Potrac et al., 2013b, 2016).

In terms of its structure, this paper is organised into four sections. Following this brief introduction, background information relating to my coaching role at Erewhon Town FC, the construction of my story, and the definition of emotion that we subscribe to in this paper are provided. My storied experiences of coaching at the club are then presented. Reflecting the sociological purpose of this paper, the discussion section provides a suggested reading of my experiences in the field (Jones, 2009). Here, complementary relational and interactionist ideas regarding emotion (Burkitt, 2014) and identity (Burkitt, 1997, 2014; Scott, 2015) are utilised as the primary sense-making tools. Importantly, we do not claim to provide a singular truth or a definitive theorisation (Jones, 2009). Instead, we use theory to reveal, clarify, and make ambiguous experience more apparent to the reader (Denison, 2016; Huggan, Nelson, & Potrac, 2015; Jones, 2009; Potrac et al., 2013a). Finally, we conclude the paper by advocating for a greater integration of emotion into ongoing and future coaching scholarship.

Constructing my story

The principals of collaborative inquiry (Jones & Ronglan, in press; Ngunjiri, Hernandez, & Chang, 2010; Toner, Nelson, Potrac, Gilbourne, & Marshall, 2012) guided the methodology employed in this study. While not a unified approach in social science research, this form of inquiry is generally understood to entail the collective, collaborative, and "critical examination of one's actions and the context of those actions" (Samaras, 2002, p. xxiv). On one level, this perspective not only requires individual reflection on personal practice, but also the reframing of these experiences to develop a conscious understanding of professional activity that goes beyond "habit, tradition, and impulse" (Samaras, 2002, p. xxiv). It also entails the sharing and joint examination of personal accounts with knowledgeable colleagues, which is seen as a valuable means for developing rich embodied and relational accounts of practice, as well as advancing our theoretical sense-making in a particular topic area (Ngunjiri et al., 2010; Samaras, 2002).

The data for this study were generated through a 12-month period of critical reflection, debate, writing, and interpretation (Haleem, Jones, & Potrac, 2003; Jones & Ronglan, in press). The process began with me, the lead author, providing a verbal presentation of the emotional nature of my work as a football coach. Following the presentation, I shared an extended written narrative of practice with my co-authors. This was informed by entries from my coaching journal, as well as my memories of the incidents, relationships, and interactions described within it. These accounts formed the basis for our monthly meetings, which took place in-person, via skype calls, and email. Our collaborative exploration of the narrative, as well as my responses to their questions, informed the ongoing refinement of the emotional experiences and social interactions contained within it. The analysis of the data entailed both emic and etic approaches (Tracy, 2013). The former was concerned with the emergent reading of the data and entailed the analytic coding of the data (Tracy, 2013). The latter entailed us seeking to make theoretical sense of my experiences. Here, we found the relational writings of Scott (2015) and Burkitt (2014) to be especially useful interpretive frameworks. Ultimately, our methodological approach entailed combining theory and narrative description in a manner that mutually enhanced and reinforced the contribution of each other (Tracy, 2013).

The context that provides the backdrop to my story is that of amateur women's football. Here, my various coaching roles were primarily concerned with designing and implementing the physical, tactical, and technical training programme, leading two training sessions per week, selecting the team, and managing the playing squad on match days (normally once a week). I was often supported in the administrative aspects of the role by a volunteer, who co-ordinated these features of team affairs. In the narrative below, this person is represented by Barry (pseudonym). While I received some remuneration from a club to cover the expenses I incurred when performing these duties, my engagement in these roles is best understood as a form of 'serious leisure' (Elkington & Stebbins, 2014). That is, in my non-work time, I chose to pursue a leisure career in an activity that I had found to be substantial, important, interesting, and fulfilling (Elkington & Stebbins, 2014). However, as my story demonstrates, my participation in this role was often characterised by a blurring of the boundaries between my professional and personal lives, as well as 'good' and 'bad' decision-making (Ritter, Powell, & Hawley, 2007; Scott, 2015)

Although the story presented in this paper is based upon recalled events, it is not beholden to them; dates, timelines, happenings, interactions, and relationships have been fashioned and dramatised (Denzin, 2014; Gearity, 2014; Holman Jones, Adams, & Ellis, 2013). Aside from my family members, the individuals featured in my story are composite characters, who have attributes like those I encountered in my various amateur football coaching roles (Bochner & Ellis, 2016). The names of other teams mentioned in my story have also been fictionalised. The emphasis is, then, as much on evocation as it is on the provision of a 'true' representation (Bochner & Ellis, 2016; Denzin, 2014; Gearity, 2014; Jones, Potrac, Haleem, & Cushion, 2006). Ultimately, however, the story seeks to illuminate "what coaching meant to me" (Jones, 2009, p. 379), especially in terms of the interconnections between my coaching identity, the emotions I experienced, and my embodied relations with others (Denison & Markula, 2003; Scott, 2015).

My story: a tale of passion and paranoia

(2nd October 2012) Beginning near the end

Me: I can't do it anymore. I'm going to tell them to start looking for someone else.

Susi: Why? I thought you were enjoying it there?

Me: I know, but I'm not feeling the buzz anymore. It's just not the same.

Susi: What's happened?

Me: Everything and nothing. I'm tired of the whole charade.

Susi: What charade?

Me: You know, the politics of it all; the false enthusiasm, the fake smiles, having to be seen to listen attentively to people talking shit! Having to be seen to care when no one seems to care in return. I know I wanted to have one more go, but I just haven't got the energy or the desire anymore.

Susi: But that's how it is. You know that. You're there to take the flak and to not complain about it. Just like any other coaching position you've had.

Me: I know. But I don't want to spend my spare time doing it anymore. It's doing my head in. Being spoken down to. Always doing a bad job from someone's perspective. Having to bottle things up all the time. I'm tired of being 'professional' and 'nice'. I want to tell people what I really think and feel! I want to be me.

Susi: Well, stop doing it then. I'll be pleased to see you at home a lot more. And it hardly makes you good company either! You're snappy and short-tempered, just like before. And you still haven't painted the walls in the baby's bedroom, despite promising you would for weeks now.

Me: I'm going to. I'm not going to put myself through it anymore.

Susi: Good! Now switch the light off and let's get some sleep.

(16th January 2012) I want one more go

I wondered how many people appreciated the angular white lines and the smell of fresh grass as much as I did. He was pointing, instructing, praising. He exchanged a 'high five' with a player. The player smiled and returned to his teammates. The events rekindled feelings from my coaching and playing pasts. Having an impact. Being valued by others. They were good times. No, they were better than that. A feeling of warmth emanated from my chest. I had an urge to be out there. That's what I wanted to be doing. I quickly reminded myself of troubled times gone before; being burned and burning others (metaphorically speaking, of course). The anxiety, guilt, and anger. But I wanted one more go; this time without the politics of the performance programme.

(23rd February 2012) Joining Erewhon Town FC: "Just do the usual things please, Paul"

"So, we're agreed that the priorities for the coming season are the adoption of a player-centred approach to the tactical and technical development of the players, an improvement on last year's disappointing results, and equitable playing time for the squad members. Just the usual things for a club like ours really, Paul," the Chair of the interview panel summarised. "Of course, we expect you to conduct yourself professionally in your dealings with players, parents, and club officials at all times. But that's taken for granted." Nods of agreement came from the remaining members of the interview panel seated alongside him. He leaned across the worn and rickety wooden table that separated me from them, with a broad smile and an outstretched hand. "Welcome aboard, Paul. It's good to have you here." "Thanks for giving me the opportunity. I'm looking forward to working with you all," I replied as we shook hands. Underneath my glossy smile and encouraging words was a strong sense of curiosity, excitement, and, indeed, anxiety. I felt beads of sweat running down my arms and my pulse increased. Contradictory thoughts reflecting my past engagements as a coach and my future hopes raced through my head: I can't wait to get started! How will events actually pan out? Things could be great here. Will they 'buy into' me as a coach? I've got a lot to offer the club. Will it be like I want it to be? Come on, Paul. Stay in the green. You want this!

(25th February 2012) First impressions: This feels comfortable

The players seemed a friendly and positive bunch. Judging by the number of BMWs and Mercedes that passed through the gates of the training ground, they hailed from 'well-heeled' families. While blessed with considerable enthusiasm, the talent on display was limited to say the least. They certainly lacked the technique, understanding, and speed of thought and movement that I had grown used to working with in the high-performance programme. Only one or two showed any potential of being able to play at a higher level. Still, I didn't mind. Their attentiveness and willingness had genuinely energised me. The feedback from players and parents had been great. By and large everyone seemed impressed with what I was doing. I enjoyed the warm smiles, the frequent 'thank yous' and compliments that I received. I felt really comfortable being there. The heat radiating through my chest confirmed my inner conversation. After all that had happened before, this mattered most to me. I'd enjoyed my can of cola after training. Caffeine, sugar, and assorted other things that are bad for my health. But I liked the sugary sweet taste. It gave me energy; made me feel good. I turned the music up loud in the car on the way home. My shoulders felt light. Life was good.

(2nd March 2012) That's Eric. Whatever you do, don't piss him off

As I tidied the balls and cones used in the session, Eric, the team sponsor, who was also a parent of one of the players, wandered over to me. "So, do you think we can win the league with this group?" he enthusiastically enquired. I began to respond with a broad and dismissive smile as I initially thought his question was humorous in its intent, but I could see by the look in his eye that he was, in fact, serious. For a split second, I was lost for words and could only laugh nervously. I regained my composure and replied, "We'll try and win every game but I think we should be realistic about what is achievable", in as reassuring a tone as I could manage. After all, they had finished last in their league by some considerable distance in the previous season. Did he not see what I saw on the training pitch? Of course, I never asked him that question. He then proceeded to spend the next 45 min informing me of the strengths and weaknesses of each player and what we could achieve with the right formation. I nodded and smiled in the right places but my jaw and facial muscles increasingly tightened as I did so. I'd met people like Eric before. I found it was easier to listen, well, to be seen to be listening at least. Really, I just wished he would stop talking. I had other things to do. Spotting a natural gap in the conversation, I seized my opportunity. "Let's see how things go, Eric," I warmly suggested. "Anyway, I've got to dash, as I need to organise some player registrations with Barry in the clubhouse. I'll see you later on." I grabbed the bag of balls and stack of cones and made my escape.

I mentioned my encounter with Eric to Barry. His response was not the one that I was hoping for. He informed me of the different priorities that Eric and the other parents had for the team. By all accounts, it seemed that informal coalition groups had formed around shared interests. Unsurprisingly, some wanted to play to win. Others wanted playing time to be strictly monitored and shared. Some felt that their daughters should be encouraged to play in a variety of positions. Others didn't. The difficulty of the situation was further added to by Barry's warning that without Eric's considerable financial generosity the club would encounter serious problems. "We can't afford to piss him off," Barry bluntly advised. Apparently, I was expected to bring some balance to these conflicting expectations. I nodded. "Well, I can only try," I stated in as upbeat a manner as I could muster. But my tightening shoulders and slightly sweating palms were symptomatic of my internal conversation. I knew where things were heading and I really didn't want to go there. I clung to the positivity of my interactions and sessions with the players. I didn't want to lose that feeling. "I'm sure it will be fine," Barry replied, giving me what I considered to be a rather knowing smile. The quiver in my stomach led me to push the pack of crisps to one side and gulp down the remainder of my can of cola. No wonder the other guy quit. "Onwards and upwards then, Barry. See you Thursday," I said with the biggest smile that I could manage. As I opened the door to my car, I wondered if Barry really bought into the bravado that I had just displayed. Or had he seen all of this before?

(16th May 2012) We're not winning but (most) people seem happy. Perfect!

Eight games in and we hadn't come close to winning a game. But there had been no complaints. In fact, only the opposite! Losing by a lot fewer goals was seen as massive progress. The effort put into transferring the lessons learnt on the training ground to match situations was clearly visible. It was great. I was getting to concentrate on what I really liked doing, which was working with the players. Trying to influence improvement. Everybody got some game time too. If I'm honest, I also enjoyed the continued praise and gratitude that I'd received from many of the parents. I always waved off the compliments and passed on the credit to the players. But I can't deny their recognition meant a great deal to me. It made me feel stronger and better as a coach and as a person. Even Eric seemed excited by the way things were going with the team. He was convinced the new formation would pay dividends in the form of a win soon. Apparently, "It's just a matter of time". But what in life isn't!

(25th May 2012) Behind a closed door

I closed the office door. I wanted some privacy. The research paper I was working on could wait for now. I grabbed a pen and opened my session planner. This was my newly established routine on Tuesdays and Thursdays. Barry had texted me to say that we would have between 12 and 16 players at training tonight. I'd have liked a full squad but that didn't matter now. I wanted it to be good. I wanted it to flow. Every detail had to be considered. It's what they expected. It's what I wanted. My fingers tingled as I compiled the order of activities and key messages to be reinforced. My mind raced forward to the session. I visualised each activity and the players' responses. Two hours later, I had addressed all my nagging concerns. I closed the session planner and returned it to my kitbag. I re-opened my office door and returned to the paper on the screen. Well, at least I tried to. As I watched the clock slowly tick round, I couldn't stop thinking about the session to come. In the end, I decided I'd get down to the training ground a bit earlier. Nothing wrong with having more time to set up. Besides, I could carry on with the paper tomorrow.

(1st June 2012) When a good result makes life more difficult

Our first point of the season! A 3–3 draw with Mornington Athletic (pseudonym) and the girls seemed really happy with their efforts. Their enthusiasm and energy made me smile and feel warm inside. They'd really bought into the team structure and patterns of play. It was making a difference. I was making a difference. That is what I wanted. As we gathered in the clubhouse for the post-game speeches, player awards, and some well-earned refreshments, the reception from Eric and some of the other parents wasn't quite as warm as I expected it to be. There were some smiles and 'well dones', but I could see that some of the parents wore a look of disappointment. I tried to figure out what was wrong. We'd drawn with a team that had resoundingly won the corresponding fixture last season. The girls had received positive feedback from the opposition players, coaches, and parents, and I'd rotated the players in order to share the playing time as equitably as I could.

Eric soon gave me the answer. "3-nil up with 20 min to go and we only get a draw, that's a real shame." His words cut me to the quick. It wasn't just what he said, it was how he said it. It was the accusatory tone of his voice and the hard look that he gave me. I felt the heat rising in my body. Despite being unsettled by his comments, I consciously maintained eye contact with him. I tried to be upbeat in my reply: "Come on, Eric, these things happen in football. But the girls seem to have enjoyed themselves and everyone got some playing time. So quite a pleasing morning all round really." Inside my head I was telling him that he was really irritating me. That he should take himself and his fantasies off for some psychiatric help. I had a telephone number he could use! "Well, I'm hoping for more from my investment in you," he retorted. "Ars*h*l*!" I muttered under my breath as I watched him return to the conversation at his table. I took a sip from my can of cola. It helped relieve the uncomfortable dryness in my throat. I rubbed the back of my neck and sighed. This should have been a high point but it wasn't. "Everything OK, Paul?" Barry asked. I almost immediately switched back into 'coach mode'. I made the smile appear. "All good, cheers, Barry. Just been a long week with work and stuff. You know how it is. Can I get you a drink?"

(14th June 2012) Who really matters? What really matters?

"I'd better call home and let people know. Will you be ok?" I asked. Susi nodded in reply. "Love you," I said as I closed the door to the doctor's office. I wanted to cry. I fumbled with my phone, almost dropping it as I searched through the directory of numbers. We'd lost our baby. I'd just assumed all would be fine. As the phone rang, the thoughts intensified in my head. Who really matters? What really matters? My conscience reminded me that I never did paint the baby's bedroom. Too busy with football stuff (again). A wave of heat flushed through my body. The dryness in my throat felt sharp, like a razor blade. "Hello, Anne. It's Paul. Listen. I've got some really bad news. I'm afraid..."

(21st July 2012) From elation to gloom in 30 s

As I pulled up the handbrake and turned off the engine I had an almost uncontrollable urge to (repeatedly) bang my head on the steering wheel. Against all the odds, the girls managed to win a game. Not only did they win, but they'd scored a goal with a counter attack move that we'd worked on in training. I should have been feeling happy, but instead I couldn't shake the cocktail of thickness in my throat and tightness in my chest. Guilt and frustration were eating at me in equal measures.

I recalled my genuine excitement as the match entered the last 30 min. My pulse raced. My voice grew increasingly hoarse. They were giving everything they had. The parents were visibly caught up in the game too. They cheered and shouted encouragement to the girls on the pitch. Seemingly from nowhere, Eric appeared next to me. "Are you going to rotate the players now, Paul?" The lack of enthusiasm in his voice left me in doubt as to what he thought. The players standing a few yards behind me were completing their warm-up. It was nearly the designated time, as it had been in previous weeks. Naturally, they wanted to be part of it. I could see the glint in their eyes. If I'm honest, I agreed with Eric. The on-field situation always deteriorated when these players were on the pitch. I didn't reply. Instead, I continued to focus my gaze on the game. Inside, my stomach was rolling and my chest tightened. I knew I would lose that day no matter what the score was.

Belying the awkward feeling in my stomach, I confidently instructed the substitutes to "Keep warm, as you'll be coming on soon". That hadn't been strictly true, as I'd decided that, this time, I'd wait for the opposition to score the equalising goal before making the changes. Given the pressure they were mounting on our goal, I couldn't help but think it would be soon. But I wanted to give the players the chance to hold out for as long as they could. I felt their efforts deserved that. After all, I know something of what it feels like to succeed after giving your all. Thoughts scatter, muscles tremble, warmth radiates through the body. Somehow you feel stronger, better, and taller. Wanting to be surrounded by family and friends. It's an amazing and powerful sensation. One to be enjoyed. I re-focused my thoughts and energies on what was happening on the field of play. Then, what seemed like only moments later, the shrill burst of the referee's whistle signalled the end of the game. For a few seconds, I felt ultra-awake, the adrenaline pumping through my body. They'd actually done it! They'd won the game! I shook hands with the opposition coach and thanked the referee for his efforts. The parents and the players on the pitch celebrated. I exchanged high fives with the player nearest me, and said, "Well done, Alice. That was brilliant!" Her wide smile and Eric's accompanying pat on the back gave me a temporary feeling of weightlessness. "Great stuff, Paul. That was really great," he added. High praise indeed!

Then it struck me. As I turned around I saw two of the substitute players and their parents already making their way to the car park. The adrenaline was replaced by a sinking feeling in my stomach. I knew something like this was likely to happen but it was still deflating. The bubble of false hope popped. "Paul, can I have a word please?" the mother of the third substitute firmly asked me. "Why didn't you put Hilary on? That's really not fair at all!" Her words only served to increase the tightening in my chest. I couldn't tell her the truth: that, on this occasion, I'd put what I thought to be the interests of the other girls ahead of Hilary's experience. I doubted that the club committee would have wanted me to share such an honest appraisal, especially with their (financial) concerns about maintaining membership numbers. "Is my daughter's development not as important as the others? What's the point in coming if she isn't going to play?" she continued, with an increasingly reddening face and a prodding finger. I could empathise with her situation. Who wouldn't? I tried to defuse the tension by apologising, explaining that I had got caught up in the flow of the game, that I was only human, and that I would make mistakes from time to time. "Yes, well, it's not bloody good enough! Do you hear?" she retorted.

As I nodded attentively to her ongoing criticisms, my teeth clenched. My pulse quickened. I wished I was able to make my feelings clear in such an unrestrained manner. Instead of nodding attentively, I wanted to ask the stuck-up 'so and so' if she had finished yet! Tell her that she should stand in my shoes and try keeping everybody happy! It's not just about Hilary, or her! As she stomped away, I saw the tears welling up in Hilary's eyes. Now that was different. A lump formed in my throat. My heart ached. I knew that I'd let her (and the other substitutes) down. That's the part of the job that I didn't like, that I didn't want to have to keep doing. You see, I also know how it feels to be excluded, to be on the periphery. That had happened to me many times and will likely do so again. Playing, coaching, working: it always feels the same. My face flushes. My skin crawls. That enveloping, horrible nauseous sensation that just won't go away. Feeling broken inside. Betrayed even. The urgent need to be alone. It isn't pleasant. It never is. "I'll see you Tuesday, Hilary. Thanks for coming and I'm really sorry that you didn't get to play today but you'll start next week. OK?" The heat and tingling in my face magnified with every word. I meant what I was saying but I'm not sure how comforting or useful such words were. Probably not at all, if truth be told.

I trudged back to the clubhouse for the post-match activities. The mood in there was very different. It was noisy. Busy. Happy. Eric was involved in an animated discussion with some of the parents, and the girls had beaming grins etched across their faces as they enjoyed the post-match sandwiches, drinks, and banter. I quickly tried to shift my melancholy mood. Why shouldn't they enjoy the moment? Why shouldn't I? I took a deep breath, composed myself, and put on that smile. Several of the parents offered to buy me a drink from the bar. I accepted with thanks, returned their smiles, offered compliments and congratulations, and laughed at their jokes. But ultimately my heart wasn't really in it. I wanted to, but I just couldn't make myself feel happy. For years I had been able to. But I couldn't do it anymore. Eric came over to where I was sitting alone. "It's great that the girls get to feel what a win is like. It has been such a long time," he said, grinning. I agreed with him as I opened a can of cola. But as I looked around the room, I felt the cold, dropping sensation of recognition intensify. I just wanted to coach. But it wouldn't be like that. It never could be. It was just like times gone before. That week I was onside with the majority but I wondered who I'd be offside with next time. My shoulders tightened and that familiar but uncomfortable feeling grew stronger. The clammy hands. The constant feeling of butterflies in the pit of my stomach. My head began to ache. I was long way from the version of coaching presented on the courses that I had attended. Thoughts raced in my mind; 'You're not good enough', 'I bet it's just you that makes such a mess of things', 'Why can't you be better at this?', 'You're letting people down again', 'Idiot!'.

I wondered what Eric would say if he knew how I truly felt. Of course, I'd never tell him or the others. Hardly the actions of a competent or so-called 'effective' coach. Not a particularly manly thing to do either. Best to say nothing. They'd only think I was odd. Eric continued his monologue on the merits of the 4–3-3 playing system. I glanced down at my watch. The ache in my head grew stronger. My attention wandered. I just wanted to get away from there, from everybody. You just don't get it do you! There's more to it than bloody formations! If only it were that simple. I'd heard enough. "Sorry, Eric. I'm just going to nip up to the bar. Can I get you anything while I'm there, mate?" I smiled. I always had to smile.

(15th August 2012) Where are their manners?

I threw the balls and cones back into my garage with unnecessary venom. The cones fell messily onto the floor but I slammed the door shut anyway. Sod it! They could be tidied up tomorrow. Who do these people think they are? Why didn't anyone tell me (or Barry)? It was embarrassing; no, humiliating! Couldn't they extend that simple courtesy? If I did the same to them, I'd be branded 'unprofessional', 'unreliable,' and probably much worse. The vein in my neck pulsed as I reflected on the farce that had played out. The planning, preparation, and an hour's drive each way to the game, and what for? Only eight players turned up! Apparently, most of the others are going to a concert. Why have they treated me in this way?

And to add further insult to injury, I knew what would happen on Tuesday night at training. There would be a group of parents expecting me to accept their apologies with good grace. Promises would be made. It wouldn't happen again. Well, until the next time at least. And I'd get that smile out again and say no harm done, that these things happen from time to time. Unlike Hilary's mum, I wouldn't be able to raise my voice, wag my finger, and be generally critical of them. Not without consequences, anyway. Coaching certainly doesn't seem to be the privilege that others had told me it is. I needed a cola.

(3rd October 2012) Thanks, but that's enough

As the girls began their warm-up, I looked around the training ground. I knew I wouldn't miss the creaky, damp, changing rooms, or the musty smell of the clubhouse bar and lounge. Nor would I mourn the end of the continual debates with Bill, the head groundsman, as to why the girls deserved to use the main training pitch as much as the boys did. But I did know that I'd miss working with the players. They'd been good company for the past year or so. Sure, there had been some ups and downs along the way, as Hilary (and others) could certainly testify to, but overall, I'd enjoyed my time with them. Hopefully, they'd enjoyed the coaching sessions and understood a bit more about the game than they did before.

That's what I wanted to help them with. That's where the warmth and energy came from. I'd taken a great deal of satisfaction from seeing the improvement and being recognised for my part in that. But I didn't want to pick teams anymore. I didn't want to do the club politics. The butterflies had gone. My shoulders felt light again. Eric and Barry joined me on the side of the pitch. "Gents, I'm glad you're here. There's no easy way to say this, but I'm going to have to stop coaching." Susi was pregnant again and I was going to paint the bedroom. That mattered. As I drove home, I turned the radio up.

(Two years later) What does he have to moan about?

The players were highly skilled. They moved the ball around the training pitch with great speed and accuracy. Concentration and enthusiasm were simultaneously etched on their faces. They were attentive to his instruction and guidance. As I leant forward on the barrier that separated me from them, I wished I was out there. Being a part of it. He'd said to bring my kit and lead part of the session. I'd politely refused. I was worried about getting back on the horse. Could I still do it? What would people think of me? More importantly, what would happen if it went well? I feared that I wouldn't be able to leave it alone. And then what?

The more I watched, the more I questioned why he had seemed a little down and tired beforehand. What did he have to moan about? Didn't he realise how good he had it here? He just needed to harden up and get on with it. I decided that I'd tell him that when we grabbed a drink after the session had finished. Then I remembered and decided that I wouldn't. I shouldn't. Hypocrite!

Making sense of my story: a suggested reading

In this section, we focus our attention on the ways in which my emotions could be understood as being experienced at the nexus of self-understanding and social relations that are "dynamic, unpredictable, and co-created" (Burkitt, 2014, p. 19). Here, the discussion is primarily inspired by the scholarly works of Burkitt (1997, 2014) and Scott (2015), which explore the issues of identity and emotion respectively. In line with their insightful arguments, we also deploy the inter-related concepts of identity commitment and salience (Stryker, 1968, 2002), role embracement (Goffman, 1961), emotional management (Burkitt, 2014; Hochschild, 1983), and role exit (Lindesmith, Strauss, & Denzin, 1999) as additional sense-making tools.

According to Burkitt (2014) and Scott (2015), identities are not constant things that people have but are, instead, entities that are continually unfolding and evolving throughout our lives. For example, Scott (2015) highlighted how our identities are created, maintained, challenged, re-invented, or exited through the process of social interaction. She posits that an identity is mediated by an individual's sense-making and responses to the symbolic meanings of other social actors' behaviours within a particular network of social relationships and interdependency (Scott, 2015). For Burkitt (2014), the self is not only socially constructed, but is also something that we feel. He noted:

> ...the I is not only a linguistic marker...it is also a deeply felt entity. Central to the formation of the self are feelings of self power that give the term 'I' its emotional animus whenever we perceive, think, and speak. The sense of 'I' has an emotional force behind it which is the 'my feeling', and if this were not the case then 'I' would be a purely linguistic expression devoid of all life and feeling. (Burkitt, 2014, p. 110)

In reflecting the position outlined above, Burkitt (2014) suggested that our feelings, emotions, and bodily sensations are "always fused with social meanings in the patterned relational weavings of our immediate social encounters" (p. 8). He believes emotion should not be regarded as a static entity as it is, in contrast, a "movement itself within relations and interactions" (Burkitt, 2014, p. 9). Instead, he argued that, within our network of social relations, "we are constantly affected by others, being moved by them to other actions, in the process of constantly feeling and thinking – being moved from one feeling or emotion to another" (Burkitt, 2014, p. 9). Importantly, Burkitt (2014, p. 16) highlighted how individuals' emotional experiences in the present cannot be separated from their "bodily disposition to feelings and thoughts stemming from past patterns and relationships" in their respective biographies. Here, past emotional (and embodied) experiences are understood to "orient, motivate, and adapt" our sense-making, choices, interactions, and behaviours (Burkitt, 2014, p. 55). From the complementary perspectives of Burkitt (2014) and Scott (2015), it could be argued that the emotional and embodied experiences of a particular role or identity are grounded in dialogical social relations.

Such theorising has considerable utility in making sense of my desire to rekindle my coaching identity and my subsequent experiences in the role. For example, having reflected upon my emotional and embodied memories of previous coaching encounters, I believed that the coaching position at Erewhon Town FC could provide opportunities for self-enrichment and self-gratification, as well as serving to enhance my self-image (Burkitt, 2014; Elkington & Stebbins, 2014). However, the achievement of these positive personal outcomes could not be understood separately from the network of relations that comprised the club setting (Crossley, 2011; Scott, 2015). Indeed, my feelings of self-worth were inextricably linked to a sense of being needed by others, of belonging, and of having an important and valued role to play within the collective activity of club life (Elkington & Stebbins, 2014; Scott, 2015). Here, I arguably demonstrated what Crossley (2006) referred to as the desire to be desired; that is, my efforts to perform well as a coach were simultaneously grounded in my past experiences, associations, and relations as a coach and my wish to obtain the approval and recognition of others in the present (Burkitt, 2014).

Importantly, the emotional-evaluative tones of others played a pivotal role in how I ultimately gave meaning to my coaching self (Burkitt, 2014; Scott, 2015). How I felt about myself and others during my time at the club was never separate from the ways others felt about me, as "expressed in their actions, looks, gestures, words, and intonations" (Burkitt, 2014, p. 111), or, indeed, how I imagined and interpreted them to feel about me. My positive readings of events and relationships were not informed by just the words of praise and gratitude that I received from others, but also by my reading of the embodied manner in which they expressed such sentiments and evaluations (Burkitt, 2014; Scott, 2015). For example, I afforded considerable symbolic value to the handshakes, smiles, and pats on the back that featured in these interactions (Scott, 2015). The rewarding features of my relationships with various contextual stakeholders were accompanied by a variety of emotions. These included enjoyment, pride, fulfilment, excitement, and elation, among others. Notably, it was the embodied experiences of these emotions, such as 'swelling' with pride, the radiating heat of happiness, the heightened senses of excitement, and the rejuvenating adrenaline rush of elation, which proved to be particularly intoxicating (Burkitt, 2014). Indeed, I still live with the legacy of these sensations, as my recalled embodied experiences inform my ongoing contemplations about a possible return to coaching in the future (Burkitt, 2014).

My embodied understanding of my coaching self featured heavily in my choice to, at times, prioritise coaching ahead of other identities and roles. For example, I frequently put the planning of coaching sessions and other club business ahead of my writing as an academic and the undertaking of household tasks. My behaviour here could, to some degree, be understood using Stryker's (1968) concepts of identity salience and commitment. The former refers to the probability of enacting an identity and its standing within a hierarchy of identities (e.g. coach, academic, partner), while the latter is concerned with the depth of commitment that an individual ascribes to a particular role that he or she performs (Scott, 2015). In a related vein, Goffman's (1961) notion of role embracement also offers some explanatory utility. For Goffman (1961), role embracement refers to the deep level of commitment and dedication that an individual affords to a given role and, relatedly, the intense concentration that is given to the execution of role-related duties (Scott, 2015). In Goffman's (1961) own words: "To embrace a role is to disappear completely into the virtual self available during the situation, to be seen fully in terms of this image, and to confirm expressively one's acceptance of it" (p. 94). This is certainly a sentiment I could subscribe to in terms of my approach to coaching for much of my tenure at the club.

However, it is important to acknowledge that my decision-making here was not an example of unfettered agency. Nor did it take place in a social, relational, and biographical vacuum (Shulman, 2017). Instead, my choices arguably reflected my subscription to wider socially constructed ideas about the 'goodness' of sport and coaching. Through my participation in various relational networks, I came to define and understand my obligations as coach in a particular way (Shulman, 2017). For example, my romanticised memories of playing sport and of being coached, as well as my understanding of sport's entwinement with contemporary notions of volunteerism, community, and being of service to others, were very much at the forefront of my thinking, feeling, and acting (Burkitt, 2014). As such, I believe I was complicit in reproducing dominant cultural (and capitalist) norms regarding 'what you should do', 'how you should feel', and 'what you should or should not show to others' (Burkitt, 2014; Ilouz, 2007; Shulman, 2017; Thoits, 2004). While not an explicit aim of this study, a consideration of the inter-relationships between emotional socialisation, the core values associated with coaching roles, and the wider power relations that shape and inform the field of human action represents a fruitful area for future inquiry (Burkitt, 2014; Zembylas, 2014). In drawing upon the work of Fineman (2008) and Tracy (2008), such inquiry might consider the "mechanisms of power and control that bear down" on coaches, the potentially "identity eroding capacity of these discourses and processes" (Fineman, 2008, p. 7), and, relatedly, their impact on coach attrition and burnout.

Unfortunately, my time at Erewhon Town FC was far from the straightforward, unifying, and positive experience that I had desired. Navigating the micro-political features of club life was, from my perspective at least, fraught with dilemmas and challenges (Jones & Wallace, 2005; Potrac & Jones, 2009a, 2009b; Potrac et al., 2013a). My efforts to pursue the often-contradictory goals of winning games, developing players, and equitably distributing playing time ultimately proved to be particularly problematic in terms of my relations with others, the emotions I experienced, and, relatedly, my thoughts about my self (Crossley, 2006; Jones & Wallace, 2005). For example, the respective criticisms that I received from Eric and Hilary's mother were not only a source of personal frustration, but they also brought a sense of tension to our ongoing relations. My embodied experiences of these encounters (e.g. heat flushing through my body, tightening of the stomach) reflected the affectively charged nature of my self and my understanding of their comments and behaviours as representing an attack upon it (Burkitt, 2014; Crossley, 2006). Similarly, the guilt and sadness I experienced regarding my choice not to allocate playing time to Hilary (and other players) in a particular game, as well as her embodied reaction to it, led me to question the 'goodness' of my coaching self (Scott, 2015). Here, the guilt emanated from my choice to engage in behaviours that I understood to violate the situational and moral codes against which I (and some others) judged my enactment of this role (Turner & Stets, 2007). Similarly, my sadness reflected my own recollections of being excluded by others in the past and what this had meant for how I had understood my self on those occasions (Burkitt, 2014). From an embodied point of view, the physical sensations included a feeling of heaviness, a tight chest, a thickness in the throat, and the inward retreat of my thoughts. The latter was also accompanied by the need to provide compensation to those whom I perceived myself to have wronged (Turner & Stets, 2007). In this case, I promised Hilary that she would start the next match.

It was my embodied experiences of these problematic situations and my subsequent reflections upon them that fuelled my questioning of the inherent pathos of the situation in which I found myself (Burkitt, 2014; Jones & Wallace, 2005).

Despite my conviction that I should be able to, it was just not possible for me to keep everybody happy all the time (or even most of the time). I concluded that, regardless of the choices I made, I would ultimately fail to live up to the levels of conduct that were valued by at least some of the parents, players, and administrators at the club (Scott, 2015). The anxiety that I subsequently experienced was rooted in my understanding of my previous problematic experiences as a coach, as well as in my anticipation of future unwanted tensions with others (Burkitt, 2014; Potrac et al., 2013a). Here, I understood such interactions to be inescapable and uncomfortable, and as having the potential to damage or spoil my coaching self (Jones, 2006; Scott, 2015). Relatedly, my gloomy outlook could also be related to my belief that I would ultimately be unable to enact the coaching role in the manner that I had longed for and which I had initially (albeit briefly) experienced in the club setting (Scott, 2015). Despite my efforts to navigate a "careful path between the demands of the occasion" (Scott, 2015, p. 84) and my personal coaching agenda, I felt defeated. In addition, I recognised that I no longer possessed the emotional stamina or desire to respond to the ongoing and fluid challenges that I believed would comprise social life at the club (Elkington & Stebbins, 2014; Hochschild, 1983; Nelson et al., 2014). My increasing disenchantment with the coaching role finally culminated in my exit from it (Scott, 2015). I arguably engaged in a process of emergent self-loss (Lindesmith et al., 1999), where my "private feelings of discomfort" culminated in my desire to be free from the role in hand (Scott, 2015, p. 166).

In addition to experiencing various and contrasting emotions in my relations with others, my role also required me to engage in emotion work (Hochschild, 1983). Specifically, this entailed hiding or showing situationally expected emotions during my encounters with others in the club setting (Nelson et al., 2014; Potrac et al., 2016). For example, at various times, I felt obliged to offer a smile to individuals while simultaneously hiding my inner feelings of frustration or anger. My engagement in such forms of surface acting (i.e. intentionally deceiving others through bodily displays to mask how we are feeling without deceiving ourselves) reflected, on one level, the club's (and wider societal) expectations of me and the service that I should provide to the players and their parents (Hochschild, 1983; Potrac & Marshall, 2011). I understood the exhibiting of anger and frustration to contravene the display rules (i.e. what, when and how overt expressions of emotion in particular situations are to occur) that the club administrators, parents, and players expected me to comply with. However, my behaviour was not solely driven by these externally imposed expectations or obligations (Hochschild, 1983; Potrac & Marshall, 2011). Instead, my outlook also reflected my own socially and biographically constructed views about how a 'good' coach ought to behave, as well as my desire to avoid 'falling out' with people at Erewhon Town FC (Potrac et al., 2016). Indeed, while I certainly felt angry and frustrated at various times, avoiding the public display of these emotions was an integral feature of my self-identification as a coach, as well as my hopes and desires regarding the nature of my relations with others (Bolton, 2004; Scott, 2015).

Finally, it would be erroneous to suggest that my emotional experiences at the club were characterised only by emotion work and inauthenticity (Burkitt, 2014; Potrac et al., 2013a, 2013b). There were many occasions where I authentically expressed my true emotions in my interactions with others. These included, for example, celebrating the team's victory with Alice and Eric and the guilt and sadness I experienced when not affording Hilary some playing time in that same game. Here, the emotions I experienced were not imposed by external feeling rules (i.e. the emotions we ought to feel in a particular situation), but were, instead, the consequence of me genuinely feeling moved by events, other people, and their emotional circumstances and predicaments (Burkitt, 2014).

Conclusion

This paper addresses the flesh and blood emotions that I experienced in my efforts to cope with the everyday demands, contingencies, and challenges of my coaching role. Through the curving of narrative time and an honest and vulnerable engagement with emotion, the text aims to do more than depict recalled personal experience (Denzin, 2014). We very much hope the reader can extract a deeper sense of meaning, especially in terms of the interconnectedness of my coaching identity, my embodied experience, and my relations with others in the club setting (Burkitt, 2014; Potrac et al., 2016; Scott, 2015). From our perspective, the significance of this paper lies not in the generalisability of my emotional experiences to the wider population of coaches. Indeed, Burkitt (2014, p. 149) argued that our engagement with the contradictions, paradoxes, and dilemmas of social life, as well as our "dialogic reflection upon conflicting impulses, means that it is not always possible to always predict in advance how people will respond". Instead, its utility is in providing a lens for considering the embodied, emotional, and relational features of coaches' lifeworlds (Jones, 2009; Potrac et al., 2013a, 2013b). We believe that a greater engagement with these topics has much to offer if our accounts of coaching are to capture better "the bodily being in the world that defines what it is to be human" (Burkitt, 2014, p. 172) than has been achieved to date. We are not advocating that emotion and embodied experience should be prioritised or, indeed, studied separately from other topics of coaching research. Rather, we hope that, wherever appropriate, future inquiry better recognises the interaction of these topics with other dynamics, issues, and priorities (e.g. learning, reflective practice, power relations, and the health and wellbeing of practitioners, among others) in sports coaching scholarship (Goodwin, Jasper, & Polletta, 2001).

Acknowledgement

The authors thank Dr. Jim Denison for his insightful and helpful feedback on an earlier version of this manuscript.

Disclosure statement

No potential conflict of interest was reported by the authors.

References

Bochner, A., & Ellis, C. (2016). *Evocative autoethnography: Writing lives and telling stories*. London: Routledge.

Bolton, S. (2004). *Emotion management in the workplace*. London: Palgrave Macmillan.

Burkitt, I. (1997). Social relationships and emotions. *Sociology, 31*, 37–55.

Burkitt, I. (2014). *Emotions and social relations*. London: Sage.

Crossley, N. (2006). The networked body and the question of reflexivity. In D. Waskul, & P. Vannini (Eds.), *Body/embodiment: Symbolic interaction and the sociology of the body* (pp. 21–34). Hampshire: Ashgate Publishing Limited.

Crossley, N. (2011). *Towards relational sociology*. London: Routledge.

Denison, J. (2016). Social theory and narrative research: A point of view. *Sport, Education and Society, 21*, 7–10.

Denison, J., & Markula, P. (2003). *Moving writing*. New York, NY: Peter Lang.

Denzin, N. (2014). *Interpretive autoethnography* (2nd ed.). London: Sage.

Elkington, S., & Stebbins, R. A. (2014). *The serious leisure perspective: An introduction*. London: Routledge.

Fineman, S. (2008). *The emotional organization: Passions and power*. Oxford: Blackwell Publishing.

Gearity, B. (2014). Autoethnography. In L. Nelson, R. Groom, & P. Potrac (Eds.), *Research methods in sports coaching* (pp. 205–216). London: Routledge.

Goffman, E. (1961). *Encounters: Two studies in the sociology of interaction*. Indianapolis, IA: Bobbs-Merrill.

Goodwin, J., Jasper, J. M., & Polletta, F. (2001). *Passionate politics. Emotions and social movements*. Chicago, IL: University of Chicago Press.

Haleem, H., Jones, R., & Potrac, P. (2003). Investigating the coach-athlete relationship: The case for autoethnography. In J. Wright (Ed.), *Researching in sport, physical and health education* (pp. 93–104). Wollongong: University of Wollongong Press.

Hochschild, A. (1983). *The managed heart: Commercialisation of human feeling*. Oakland, CA: University of California Press.

Holman Jones, S., Adams, T., & Ellis, C. (2013). *Handbook of autoethnography*. London: Routledge.

Huggan, R., Nelson, L., & Potrac, P. (2015). Developing micropolitical literacy in professional soccer: A performance analyst's tale. *Qualitative Research in Sport, Exercise and Health, 7*, 504–520.

Ilouz, E. (2007). *Cold intimacies: The making of emotional capitalism*. Cambridge: Cambridge University Press.

Jones, R. (2006). Dilemmas, maintaining "face", and paranoia: An average coaching life. *Qualitative Inquiry, 12*, 1012–1021.

Jones, R. (2009). Coaching as caring (the smiling gallery): Accessing hidden knowledge. *Physical Education and Sport Pedagogy, 14*, 377–390.

Jones, R., Armour, K., & Potrac, P. (2004). *Sports coaching cultures: From practice to theory.* London: Routledge.

Jones, R., Edwards, C., & Viotto Filho, I. (2016). Activity theory, complexity and sports coaching: An epistemology for a discipline. *Sport, Education and Society, 21*, 200–216.

Jones, R., Potrac, P., Cushion, C., & Ronglan, L. T. (Eds.). (2011). *The sociology of sports coaching.* London: Routledge.

Jones, R., Potrac, P., Haleem, H., & Cushion, C. (2006). Exposure by association: Maintaining anonymity in auto-ethnographical research. In S. Fleming, & F. Jordan (Eds.), *Ethical issues in leisure research* (pp. 45–62). Eastbourne: Leisure Studies Association.

Jones, R., & Ronglan, L.T. (2017). What do coaches orchestrate? Unravelling the 'quiddity' of practice. *Sport, Education and Society.* Advance online publication. doi: 10.1080/13573322.2017.1282451

Jones, R., & Wallace, M. (2005). Another bad day at the training ground: Coping with ambiguity in the coaching context. *Sport, Education and Society, 10*, 119–134.

Kelchtermans, G. (2005). Teachers' emotions in educational reforms: Self-understanding, vulnerable commitment and micropolitical literacy. *Teaching and Teacher Education, 21*, 995–1006.

Lindesmith, A., Strauss, A., & Denzin, N. (1999). *Social psychology.* Thousand Oaks, CA: Sage.

Nelson, L., Potrac, P., Gilbourne, D., Allanson, A., Gale, L., & Marshall, P. (2014). Thinking, feeling, acting: The case of a semi-professional soccer coach. *Sociology of Sport Journal, 19*, 19–40.

Ngunjiri, F., Hernandez, K., & Chang, H. (2010). Living autoethnography: Connecting life and research. *Journal of Research Practice, 6*(1). Article E1. Retrieved from http://jrp.icaap.org/index.php/jrp/article/view/241/186

Potrac, P., & Jones, R. (2009a). Micro-political workings in semi-professional football coaching. *Sociology of Sport Journal, 26*, 557–577.

Potrac, P., & Jones, R. (2009b). Power, conflict and co-operation: Towards a micro-politics of coaching. *Quest, 61*, 223–236.

Potrac, P., Jones, R., Gilbourne, D., & Nelson, L. (2013a). Handshakes, BBQs, and bullets: A tale of self-interest and regret in football coaching. *Sports Coaching Review, 1*, 79–92.

Potrac, P., Jones, R., Purdy, L., Nelson, J., & Marshall, P. (2013b). Coaches, coaching, and emotion: A suggested research agenda. In P. Potrac, W. Gilbert, & J. Denison (Eds.), *The Routledge handbook of sports coaching* (pp. 235–246). London: Routledge.

Potrac, P., & Marshall, P. (2011). Arlie Russell Hochschild: The managed heart, feeling rules, and emotional labour: Coaching as an emotional endeavour. In R. Jones, P. Potrac, C. Cushion, & L. T. Ronglan (Eds.), *The sociology of sports coaching* (pp. 54–66). London: Routledge.

Potrac, P., Nelson, L., & O'Gorman, J. (2016). Exploring the everyday realities of grass-roots football coaching: Towards a relational perspective. *Soccer and Society, 17*, 910–925.

Purdy, L., & Potrac, P. (2016). Am I just not good enough? The creation, development and questioning of a high-performance coaching identity. *Sport, Education and Society, 21*, 778–795.

Ritter, J., Powell, D., & Hawley, T. (2007). Takin' it to the streets: A collaborative self-study into social studies. *Social Studies Research and Practice, 2*(3), 1–17.

Samaras, A. (2002). *Self-study for teacher educators. Crafting a pedagogy for educational change.* New York, NY: Peter Lang Publishing.

Scott, S. (2015). *Negotiating identity: Symbolic interactionist approaches to social identity.* Cambridge: Polity Press.

Shulman, D. (2017). *The presentation of self in contemporary society.* London: Sage.

Stryker, S. (1968). Identity salience and role performance. *Journal of Marriage and the Family, 30*, 558–564.

Stryker, S. (2002). *Symbolic interactionism: A social structural version.* Caldwell, NJ: Blackburn Press.

Thoits, P. (2004). Emotion norms, emotion work, and social order. In A. Manstead, N. Frijda, & A. Fischer (Eds.), *Feelings and emotions: The Amsterdam symposium* (pp. 359–378). Cambridge: Cambridge University Press.

Thompson, A., Potrac, P., & Jones, R. (2015). 'I found out the hard way': Micro-political workings in professional football. *Sport, Education & Society, 20*, 976–994.

Toner, J., Nelson, L., Potrac, P., Gilbourne, D., & Marshall, P. (2012). From 'blame' to 'shame' in a coach–athlete relationship in golf: A tale of shared critical reflection and the re-storying of narrative experience. *Sports Coaching Review, 1*, 67–78.

Tracy, S. (2008). Power, paradox, social support, and prestige: A critical approach to addressing correctional officer burnout. In S. Fineman (Ed.), *The emotional organization: Passions and power* (pp. 27–43). Oxford: Blackwell Publishing.

Tracy, S. (2013). *Qualitative research methods: Collecting evidence, crafting analysis, communicating impact.* Malden, MA: Wiley-Blackwell.

Turner, J., & Stets, J. (2007). Moral emotions. In J. Stets, & J. Turner (Eds.), *Handbook of the sociology of emotion* (pp. 544–566). New York, NY: Springer.

Zembylas, M. (2014). The place of emotion in teacher reflection: Elias, Foucault, and critical emotional reflexivity. *Power and Education, 6*, 210–222.

Sport coaches' experiences of athlete injury: the development and regulation of guilt

Laura Ann Martinelli, Melissa Catherine Day and Ruth Lowry

ABSTRACT

This study sought to examine coaches' experiences of guilt in the specific context of athlete injury. In-depth, semi-structured interviews were utilised to generate data. Our analysis suggested that not only was guilt a commonly felt emotion, but was also one that that the participants attempted to regulate. The coaches' stories were primarily, although not exclusively, interrogated using the psychological theorising concerning trauma-related guilt. We conclude the paper by making connections to, and from, the coaches' experiences of guilt with existing critiques of the prevailing deontological approach used to define what it means to be a 'good' sport coach. Here, we suggest that dominant perspectives in coach education may be instrumental in entrenching coaches' experience of guilt.

Introduction

Research on the psychological consequences of athletic injury has predominantly focused on the perspectives and experiences of the injured athlete (e.g. Grindstaff, Wrisberg, & Ross, 2010; Walker, Thatcher, & Lavallee, 2007; Wiese-Bjornstal, 2010). While the coach has been identified as an important member of an injured athlete's support network, there has been little consideration of the psychological ramifications that athlete injury may have for coaches (Bianco, 2001; Corbillon, Crossman, & Jamieson, 2009; Robbins & Rosenfeld, 2001). In an effort to address this discrepancy, Day, Bond, and Smith (2013) produced a narrative case study of two national level trampoline coaches, who were present during a training session in which one of their athletes sustained an open leg fracture. Their study demonstrated that even amongst coaches of the same sport who had witnessed the same injury, subsequent reactions and experiences could vary. For example, while one coach attempted to downplay the severity, the other believed the injury posed a significant threat to the athlete's physical integrity and career. Despite these early differences, both coaches recalled episodes of involuntarily re-experiencing the event that were trigged upon re-entering the environment in which the incident had occurred and having contact with the injured athlete. Hence, there was considerable effort exerted by the coaches to avoid conversations about the injury within the training environment. From these findings, Day et al. (2013) suggested a link between coaches' experiences of sporting injury and the symptoms of post-traumatic stress.

Post-traumatic stress is a popular conceptualisation of the way a person's subjective well-being, balance of affective states, and overall satisfaction and happiness may be compromised by an adverse event (Joseph & Linley, 2005). Indeed, the oscillation between intrusions (e.g. re-experiencing) and avoidance of event-related stimuli after witnessing (i.e. vicarious exposure) or learning about (i.e. indirect exposure) an event involving actual or threatened serious injury, are recognised as part of a constellation of post-traumatic stress symptoms (Diagnostic and Statistical Manual of Mental Disorders [DSM-5], American Psychiatric Association [APA], 2013; Friedman, 2013). In this regard, Day et al. (2013) highlighted how such avoidance was found to restrict coaches' abilities to receive social support, a strong predictor of post-traumatic stress symptoms (Ozer, Best, Lipsey, & Weiss, 2008).

For some readers, the proposition that sport injury may be conceptualised as a potentially traumatic event for coaches may be unconvincing, especially given that injury can be a regular and perhaps normalised part of working life as a sports coach (Frisch, Seil, Urhausen, Croisier, Lair, & Theisen, 2009; Mattila, Parkkari, Koivusilta, Kannus, & Rimpelä, 2009). However, in line with a schema-based theoretical perspective towards the development of post-traumatic stress (Janoff-Bulman, 1992; Joseph & Linley, 2005; Park, 2010), an event may be psychologically traumatic because it has posed a meaningful threat to a person's individualised yet global beliefs and goals. For example, even where a coach appears knowledgeable of the risk of injury, its occurrence can be psychologically traumatic for two reasons. Firstly, it may deeply contradict existing understandings about why and how such injuries happen. Secondly, it can also impact upon individual self-perceptions in terms of the extent to which he or she believed themselves to be a good, moral, willing and/or capable coach. This suggests that the traumatic meaning of sport injury resides not in an objective assessment of severity and prevalence of an event, but in the coach's subjective appraisal of that event and the way in which it contradicts their expectations about the occurrence of injury and the self (Gabert-Quillen, Fallon, & Delahanty, 2011). Simply put, the more the coach's initial appraisal of the event is discrepant with his or her pre-existing beliefs and goals connected to injury in sport, the greater the level of distress to the individual's subjective well-being will be.

Of recent debate within the mainstream psychological literature is the emotional content to psychological trauma. Older conceptualisation of a traumatic event (APA, 1994) required the individual to have experienced fear, helplessness or horror at the time of one's exposure to an event involving actual or threatened serious injury, in order to qualify as having been exposed to a traumatic event. Yet this peri-traumatic emotional configuration of fear, helplessness or horror has been removed from current conceptualisations of a traumatic event because of mounting evidence that post-traumatic symptoms could also develop if a person had experienced alternative peri-traumatic emotions or even emotional numbing whilst in the process of witnessing or learning about such an event (Bovin & Marx, 2001; Friedman, 2013; Hathaway, Boals, & Banks, 2011). Consequently, in the most recent conceptualisation of post-traumatic stress offered by the DSM-5 (APA, 2013), a new symptom category was created to exclusively address negative alterations in mood and cognition. This indicated that a persistent negative emotional state which may involve fear, horror, anger, shame, or guilt could be experienced as part of one's response to experiencing, witnessing or learning about an event involving actual or threatened serious injury to qualify as having been exposed to a traumatic event.

Relative to the state of literature that conceptualises post-traumatic responses as a predominantly fear-based phenomenon, attention to trauma-related guilt is sparse. It is generally agreed that guilt is characteristically an intense and unpleasantly valenced affective state, accompanied by beliefs that one should have thought, felt or acted differently (Blum, 2008; Pugh, Taylor & Berry, 2015). Thus, guilt constitutes a sense of wrongdoing because of the perceived connection between one's actions or inactions and a negative outcome. Although the experience of guilt following trauma has been a point of some theoretical and empirical interest, there is no conceptual consensus on this topic. For example, Lee, Scragg, and Turner (2001) argued that guilt may be a disabling emotional response to a trauma event because it signals that the self is being experienced in a negative way. Blum (2008) meanwhile portrays guilt as a maladaptive emotion underpinning psychopathologies. Conversely, others address the more adaptive qualities of this emotion. In this regard, Baumeister, Stillwell, and Heatherton (1994) argued that guilt is a social emotion that serves to strengthen relationships by reducing the frequency of transgressions against others. Similarly, Carnì, Petrocchi, Del Miglio, Mancini, and Couyoumdjian (2013) described guilt as a moral emotion that helps individuals adjust to, and adopt, cultural norms for the purpose of social survival. There is also a lack of consensus over the precise relationship between guilt and the development of post-traumatic stress. Here, whereas the DSM-5 (APA, 2013) situates guilt as one of a constellation of post-traumatic stress symptoms, Lee et al. (2001) and Kubany and Watson (2003) have forwarded models of trauma-related guilt that conceptualize the emotion as constitutive of a type of post-traumatic response that drives other symptoms of post-traumatic stress (Browne, Trim, Myers, & Norman, 2015).

Given the different trajectories that guilt might have, and the lack of research undertaken to understand this emotion in the working lives of coaches, we explored coaches' experience of guilt in the specific context of athletic injury. As such, the current study provides an initial qualitative insight into the multifaceted development and regulation of guilt among coaches. In doing so, it illustrates the different ways that guilt may be embodied and subsequently managed by coaches in response to athletic injury. Such knowledge holds the potential to make an important contribution to the literature concerning trauma-related guilt and the emotional landscape of sport coaching more generally (Potrac et al., 2013).

Methods

Participants and sampling

Ten sports coaches (6 male, 4 female) aged between 19 and 69 years were recruited. The participants had between 4 and 33 years coaching experience in their chosen sports. These included rugby (n = 2), football (n = 3), hockey (n = 2), basketball (n = 1), equestrian dressage (n = 1), and skiing (n = 1). The participants coached in a variety of settings (e.g. grassroots, recreational, and high performance). All but one had obtained either a level one, two or three coaching qualification in the UK. To facilitate the recruitment of coaches with a variety of experiences of sport injury, three sampling criteria were used. The criteria were informed by the definitions of a reportable sports injury recommended by the surveillance literature (Wiese-Bjornstal, 2010) and required the coaches to clarify if they had witnessed an injury that: (i) occurred during an organised session of training or competition, (ii) required immediate medical attention, and (iii) prevented the injured individual from resuming their participation in the organised session of training or competition. It is important to note that the injury criteria detailed above is indicative of an inclusive and subjective approach towards injury severity that reflected the coaches' sense making regarding severity of injuries (Bianco, 2001). The participants, as well as the individuals and organisations portrayed in their stories, have been given pseudonyms. This study received formal approval from the institutional ethics committee.

Interviews

Each coach participated in two semi-structured interviews that were conducted by the lead author. The semi-structured interview method entails the use of flexible, open-ended questions to explore the participants' thoughts, feelings and experiences (Sparkes & Smith, 2014). Following the completion of initial pilot work, the interview guide for the main study addressed the following topics: (a) entrance into coaching, (b) perspectives towards injury, (c) contextual details surrounding the injury event, (d) immediate responses to the injury, (e) long-term responses to the injury, and (f) further evaluations of the experience. In drawing upon narrative methodology, open-ended questions were utilised in order to encourage the interviewee to produce chronological accounts of their experiences (Smith &

Sparkes, 2009). Indeed, a distinguishing feature of the narrative approach is its attention to the forging of temporal connections between the different events in the generation of meaning (Elliot, 2005; Polkinghorne, 1991, 1995; Squire, 2008). Furthermore, in accordance with schema-based theory (e.g. Day, 2012; Joseph & Linley, 2005), some questions also sought to explore the interviewees' beliefs and goals connected to injury in sport and the extent to which these were discrepant with, or changed by, a particular experience of an athlete's injury.

The first interviews lasted between 64 and 241 min, and the second interviews lasted between 32 and 189 min. The decision to cease the interviewing process in this study was also informed by on-going discussions between myself, the principal researcher, and a senior colleague, who acted as a "critical-friend" (Sparkes & Smith, 2014, p. 182). In these conversations, I was encouraged to critically reflect on the quality of the developing data in relation to the research aims, as well as my ability to cope with the data. The latter of which could be termed "researcher-saturation".

Data analysis

The transcribed audio recordings of the interviews were analysed in a manner consistent with a holistic-content approach outlined by Lieblich, Tuval-Mashiach, and Zilber (1998). The advantage of taking a narrative and holistic approach to analysis is that it avoids an excessive dissection of the interview transcripts that would otherwise result in decontextualized reading of the data (Riessman, 2008). Towards this end, the initial phase of analysis entailed engaging in empathetic readings of the data and documenting initial and global impressions. Here, for example, it was noted here that there was a tendency amongst the coaches to more comfortably elaborate on their evaluations of others' responses to a given sport injury rather than their own. Equally, moments of emotionality within the participants' stories of injury were typically short-lived and tended to interspace more analytical and procedural reflections pertaining to the incident. Within these moments of introspection, the coaches experience of guilt was highlighted as a prominent emotion, and therefore became a "special foci of content or themes" for further analysis (Lieblich et al., 1998, p. 63). The final two steps of the analysis involved coding and tracking the development of this theme throughout the data set (Lieblich et al., 1998). Relevant extracts were then examined and clustered. From this point onwards, writing was employed as a method of analysis to develop and refine interpretations of composite themes (Richardson & St. Pierre, 2005). Furthermore, throughout this process of analysis-by-writing, existing literature was regularly engaged with to make further sense of the data and to organise interpretations. In doing so, novel understandings were put forward whilst efforts were also made to connect coaches' responses to injury with mainstream theoretical propositions regarding the development and management of guilt following adverse events (Kubany & Watson, 2003).

Judging this study

The current study was informed by an interpretivist philosophy, which regards research as a shared and interactive process between the researcher and participant(s) (Denzin & Lincoln, 2008; Lincoln, Lynham, & Guba, 2011; Willig, 2008). The current study was also informed by a narrative methodology. In line with Smith and Sparkes (2009), a narrative approach to research is based on several principles, the first of which contends that a fundamental condition of being human is our propensity to actively construe meaning out of life's events and happenings. Indeed, as a species we are characterised by our endeavour to make sense of and thus give meaning to otherwise random, unrelated and inconsequential experiences. Narrative methodology therefore argues that meaning is not something that inherently resides in the events and happenings; rather it is something a person interprets and continually revises over time (Smith & Sparkes, 2009). A second principle advocated by narrative methodology is the contention that meaning is achieved by humans through the use of narratives and in the act of storytelling (Andrews, 2000). Humans are characterised by an aptitude for narrative and to tell stories, and it is through our engagement with narratives and storytelling that we make sense of our lives (Kramp, 2004).

In reflecting the interpretivist philosophy underpinning this work, readers are invited to judge its quality in relation to the following non-foundational criteria (Smith, Sparkes & Caddick, 2014).

- Do the data extracts provide a new or different understanding of the emotional experiences of coaches in the context of athletic injury?
- Is appropriate literature used in ways that helps to further unpack and explore the possible meanings of the coaches' experiences?
- How well are multiple realities and storylines negotiated?

Results and discussion

Most prominent to the emotional landscape of the coaches' stories of sporting injury was the issue of guilt. This finding is unpacked and explored in relation to (a) the development of guilt and (b) the regulation of guilt.

The development of guilt

For many of the participants, the experiencing of guilt was inevitable after witnessing a serious injury to an athlete in their charge. For example, Lisa demonstrated this when recounting an injury that occurred during her first paid coaching session as an equestrian coach. In her own words:

> ... I did think at that point he'd broken his arm ... yeah that was quite a traumatic experience and I *always* remember that that *first* one, there'll have been hundreds since

> then but I always remember that first one ... I don't know how it is in other sports but certainly in equestrian, I always feel guilty if one of my riders has got hurt. ... you're responsible for the safety of the people that you're coaching and that responsibility is really hammered into you, and that guilt can be quite horrible afterwards ... there's no difference to your realisation of what *can* happen, it slams you pretty much in the gut ... whatever happens in that arena is your responsibility, so it's *that*, even if it's not your fault, it's your responsibility ...

Interestingly, in stating that she 'always' felt guilty whenever her riders sustained injuries, Lisa suggested that there was an inevitable and perhaps customary level of guilt after an injury. Lisa perceived that guilt was not necessarily a consequence of a recognisable coaching action that had caused the injury (even if it's not your fault). Instead, her guilt stemmed from her position within a hierarchy of responsibility that compelled her to feel accountable for the safety of the individuals in her charge. This outlook reflected the work of Kubany and Manke (1995), who argued that the probability of experiencing trauma-related guilt is heightened by one's social position being confused as having the capacity and power to control all outcomes.

While Lisa described immediate guilt, Andrew explained that his guilt was a product of post-event reflection. In his own words:

> Whether the coach is responsible or not, he [sic] is a definite part of any of injury because it is most likely that he would have been there when his athlete got injured and he will have had *thoughts* or feelings somewhere down the line (pauses) about *guilt*. I don't mean that he's guilty but as a coach he will be thinking 'could I have done this, could I have done that' and we can always look on with hindsight; it's a wonderful thing ...

According to Andrew, it is the coach's natural reflection in the aftermath of the incident that explains why guilt is an inevitable experience. Through the use of imaginary scenarios, Andrew considered courses of action different to those that were taken and which might have had a positive impact upon the extent or likelihood of the injury sustained. According to Kubany and Watson (2003), such cognitive activity is conducive to guilt, as it generates beliefs about the foreseeability and preventability of a negative event. Importantly, Kubany and Watson (2003) warned that such beliefs may be informed by hindsight bias (knowledge of the outcome), thereby increasing the magnitude of the guilt experienced. This knowledge of the outcome can prompt imaginary alternative actions to be perceived as options that were actually available to the coach. Andrew's comments, therefore, alert us that guilt may result from a coach's post-injury reflections, particularly if the coach is not able to distinguish between pre-event and post-event knowledge. Coaches are increasingly encouraged to be reflective (Knowles, Borrie, & Telfer, 2005), yet the emotional repercussions of the reflective process and the possibility of hindsight bias have not been acknowledged. From our perspective, this represents an important line of inquiry for scholars in the sports coaching community.

Patrick, a 26-year-old football coach, offered an alternative account of guilt. For Patrick, guilt was immediate but cultivated through multiple interrelated thoughts about an injury. He stated:

> … the ground was hard…the surface was tricky, wasn't dangerous but it was tricky … she [the player] tried turning away from the collision I believe, and either got her feet stuck in the ground or her body turned too quickly for her legs … I just felt guilt from, from the first minute,…it was just the guilt … it wasn't too much panic, it was more a case of this game perhaps shouldn't be playable … that was the initial thought that should we have actually kept this game on today? … that was what was a bit more painful for me because I had an influence on the surface. So, I'd spoken to the groundsman, the officials and as a committee we decided to keep the match on … so that's why there's that added sense of personal responsibility ...

In permitting a competitive match to take place on a 'tricky' surface, a causal link was created between his actions and the occurrence of the injury, because, for Patrick, the most obvious and proximal cause of the injury was the questionable surface. Adding to the magnitude of guilt experienced by this coach, was his realisation that the pre-match discussions and subsequent decisions made about the pitch could have been 'better'. Patrick concluded that he had decided about the safety of the pitch from the perspective of a player rather than from that of a coach. He noted:

> Most incidents happen, there's nothing prior … to the incident, that could have been managed better but it wasn't. I looked at it [the pitch] as if, well, I'd play on it … because I would, but would I play on it safely? I don't know. Looking back now, it's like poor decision …

Patrick regretted that he had appraised the safety of the pitch in accordance with his personal willingness as a player. Here, his experience corresponded with a particular cognition said to contribute to the magnitude of trauma-related guilt; specifically, a perceived insufficient justification for actions taken (Lee et al., 2001; Kubany and Watson, 2003). Thus, in believing that one's actions or inactions connected to a negative event lack sufficient rationale or logic, the risk of experiencing guilt increases. Kubany and Manke (1995) further proposed that perceived insufficient justification and thus guilt can be heightened when one focuses on the positive outcomes that might have taken place if an alternative action had been embarked upon. As Patrick described:

> … she was playing really well … she was literally leading the line, causing problems and then it just happened … it shouldn't have happened to a player like this who's twenty years old, who is a good player, going places …

Thus, the injured player's good performance on the day and her potential to have a promising football career also contributed to Patrick's guilt. As such, the coach's understanding of the injured athlete's actual or potential sporting ability could be a factor that heightens or lessons guilt.

Patrick's experiences overlap with comments from Jerry, a rugby coach, who elaborated on the circumstances surrounding an injury that would be more likely to arouse an emotional response from him. He noted:

> … the only other thing which would be *shocking* is the player involved in terms of knowing their history. So, if they've *just* returned from injury and you feel for them because it couldn't have been worse luck, or a player who's got a trial or wanting to go on to bigger and better things, them being *set back*, they'd be the only things then which would emotionally trigger a reaction for me …

Although Jerry did not explicitly talk about guilt as an emotion constitutive of his experience of sport injury, there was an important recognition that his knowledge of the injured athlete could make the incident more or less emotionally potent. Similarly, Eleanor described how her negative perception of an injured individual had negated her emotional involvement in that player's injury. More specifically, Eleanor had dismissed the player's injury symptoms that would eventually be confirmed as a punctured lung, so much so that it was some hours before the injured player received medical care. Eleanor noted:

> … one of the most serious injuries we've ever had … now I didn't talk about him last week [laughs] and my reason for that is probably what I'm going to try and justify here on personality things. He was a player who moaned at every opportunity, and I mean that in terms of feeling like he was hard-done-by in life as a whole … he was nowhere near the level that he should have been and quite frankly, without sounding really like I'm treading on him, never will be bless him …

Eleanor's negative evaluation of the player appeared to quash the possibility of experiencing guilt. One's knowledge of the injured individual has been suggested as a pre-trauma factor that can have a meaningful influence on the way any traumtic incident is construed (Lerias & Byrne, 2003). Moreover, Kubany and Watson (2003) proposed that close physical and personal proximity with the injured individual should increase the probability of trauma-related guilt. In line with such theorising, Eleanor's negative regard for the injured athlete inferred little personal proximity between herself and the injured athlete. Such a relationship arguably prevented Eleanor from experiencing guilt in response to an incident in which the welfare of the injured athlete was essentially neglected.

The contention that a positive relationship exists between the coach having a close physical and personal proximity with the injured athlete and the magnitude of guilt was, however, contradicted by two of the coaches' stories of injury. Jade, a hockey coach of an under twelve team at a community-based sports club, recounted an injury sustained by a child:

> … Jonathon, he's my *best* defender … a boy [opposition player] hit the ball really really hard … it would have been a great shot, but Jonathon was there and it hit him *right* in the knee … he was on the floor, he was crying. I like Jonathon because he's like me as a player, I see myself in him … I guess it was just bad timing of how he [Jonathon] ran to the player and you can't really influence … actually it was a good thing that Jonathon went towards that player with the ball … Jonathon definitely did the right thing in going towards him to get the ball …

The injured child in Jade's story was portrayed in a positive light, yet her story was entirely absent of explicit or implicit inferences of guilt. This may be because Jade regarded the child's actions as unrelated to her coaching. Yet, as previously established through Lisa's comments, a coach does not always need to recognise such a connection to experience guilt. In an alternative story of sport injury that also challenges Kubany and Watson (2003) hypothesis, Lisa spoke of a former rider's spinal cord injury:

> … you can even feel guilty about people that you coach who injure themselves when it's *nothing* to do with you. So, it's not in your session, and it's not in your [yard], but because you've *taught* them and they go out and do something else, and then they get injured, there is a little creeping feeling of guilt … I have a lady that I taught for about four or five years, who took her horse out hunting, fell off her horse and fractured her spine, is in a wheelchair for the rest of her life now, and that happened about eight weeks ago maybe … the awful thing is she's no great friend … I've never been round her house … I hadn't coached her for about six weeks because she'd moved yards and she'd gone quite a long way away from us and she'd actually changed coach …

Lisa's comments are particularly novel because they document the possibility of slowly developing guilt, even when detached from the athlete. This particular case may be explained in relation to the life changing injuries faced by this athlete. As Lisa explained:

> I still can't help *feeling* it, even though rationally I know it's totally ridiculous but you still kind of feel 'oh if only I'd coached her a little bit better', would she have sat up straight, would she have actually ridden that jump a bit better, would she have not fallen off …

Lisa then, still saw herself as an inextricable part of her former rider's good or bad performances through the part she had played in helping the rider acquire or develop techniques that may be used to evade injury. This is in agreement with Kubany and Manke (1995), who outlined that an exaggerated sense of personal responsibility for an event and/or its outcomes is one of several thinking errors that increase the person's aptitude to experience guilt. Lisa's story suggests a need amongst some coaches for guidance with respect to responsibility boundaries, while her account also prompt debate about where responsibility lines should be drawn in relation to both athlete and coach welfare (Cassidy, Jones, & Potrac, 2009; Simon, 2013).

The regulation of guilt

For those coaches who had identified guilt in the aftermath of a sport injury, there were differences in their efforts to regulate their thoughts and affective states. Salient to the stories offered by both Patrick and Lisa was their avoidance of the injured individual. Patrick, for example, conveyed a desire to keep a physical distance between himself and the injured individual. He described:

> I didn't even want to go to the hospital because I felt that much guilt. If it was professional, I would have gone straight to the hospital … I would have been there straight away after the game with Ashley … I just couldn't go, with it being a bit more personal, I felt I must get out of this … I didn't know Ashley's reaction to maybe (pauses) her opinion on the game being on or off. I didn't want to cause friction or confrontation …

Patrick's description echoes the findings of Day et al. (2013), who reported that coaches found it emotionally distressing to be in contact with injured athletes. Such avoidance strategies have also been reported from the perspective of the athlete, with injured swimmers suggesting that their attempts to communicate with coaches leaving them feeling overlooked and pushed aside (Abgarov, Jeffery-Tosoni, Baker, & Fraser-Thomas, 2012). Patrick's comments, however, highlighted that a coach's absence can result from anticipated response, which in turn becomes a source of guilt for the coach. This corroborates Kubany and Watson (2003) multi-dimensional model of guilt in which avoidance signifies one's need for short-term respite from the emotion.

Failing to visit the injured individual could, however, be a problematic experience. Patrick indicated that in failing to visit the injured player in hospital, he was failing to act in accordance with what would have been a more professional response to these circumstances. Similarly, Lisa's inability to be in the presence of the rider who had sustained a spinal cord injury was problematic because it deeply contradicted her sense of self:

> I can't quite face going to see her yet. It's really odd because I am quite a stoical person you know; I'll shove guts back into horses that have been, that are damaged … I'm surprised at how reluctant I'm being about going to see her really … I would have thought I would have been fine with that and there's so many things that I am fine with but I think 'oh no I'll just put that off for another week' and 'I'll just put that off for another week …'

By avoiding the injured individual, Lisa acted in an unfamiliar way. Both Lee et al. (2001) and Kubany and Watson (2003) regarded a departure from a valued way of acting as a determinant of guilt. By using avoidance, Patrick and Lisa made little progress in gaining respite from their experiences of guilt. Consequently, both attempted to use a combination of avoidance and tentative approach. Taking small steps to contact the injured player, Patrick inquired about her via teammates, whilst also sending gifts:

> … I made phone calls and texts instead because I didn't want to completely obviously reject her … I can't remember if I spoke to *her* specifically the next day but it would have been to somebody at the hospital, one of the other players … I managed to get some training kit from her favourite football team [and] a card for everyone to sign … that's what I think I'd want. So yeah more than anything it was just to reiterate that you're not forgotten …

Making contact with the injured player via others and by sending gifts was a safer mode of regulating guilt for Patrick in the short-term. Eventually, on seeing the injured athlete, Patrick sought her forgiveness:

> … she is a bubbly character, she was laughing, joking about it and it obviously helped. … I apologised to her, and she was saying of course it's not your fault, it happens, and *that* kind of thing really. … for me, as a coach, it was perfect to see her again and yeah it massively helped to have someone like her, who dealt with it just laughing it off … and just reiterating 'no everything's good, I'm okay, it's happened …

Forgiveness from others is an important way in which guilt related thoughts may be more permanently reduced and even eliminated (Kubany and Watson, 2003). Patrick's story highlights that the first meeting between an injured athlete and a coach experiencing guilt can be crucial to changing the coach's emotional landscape in the aftermath of an injury.

Other accounts of regulating guilt involved different trajectories, with one coach encouraging an injured athlete to take legal action. Andrew was acting as the assistant coach at a training camp for elite disability skiers when an athlete (Claude) with an existing amputation to the right limb sustained several fractures to his left limb. Prior to the accident, Andrew had noticed that several of the slalom poles were not properly drilled into the piste and had relayed this information to the head coach, who subsequently informed the skiers about the risk. In the following quotation, Andrew spoke of his need for reparation:

> … I could see that Claude may not walk again. I mean you have to think about that because it's a broken leg. It was a bad break, three broken bones … it upset me that we should have *avoided* it, it *was* avoidable … I was a part of the decision so I was just as culpable as the head coach … what we did was wrong. It happened and you can't change it, but you can possibly make reparation somewhere, you can try and make it a bit easier … my reaction was to encourage Claude to sue me and the head coach. Claude said, 'no I can't', but I continued to encourage him to sue me for a year. It may sound odd to you, but for me, that was quite important … I was aware that it would be a problem for me if Claude did sue me because it would have been in the papers, but I felt that it was the right thing to do and I needed Claude to know that …

Andrew encouraged his athlete to take legal action, which would have involved a claim of negligence being brought against him (James, 2013). The initiation of legal proceedings could have jeopardised Andrew's reputation and career as a sports coach. However, he perceived this to be the best way to make amends for his perceived error and to address his feelings of guilt.

Interestingly, for other coaches, the threat of legal action was problematic, inciting fear rather than the alleviation of guilt. For example, Lara stated:

> … you have to look at liability and things as well, and don't get me wrong, I was completely worried about it … it was scary like, I said you think about the person who's injured and then it's kind of the after thought of, especially in that situation like oh my God, I'm in so much trouble for this, like what if someone tried to sue me …

This situation is perhaps unsurprising given the compensation culture said to currently exist within sport (James, 2013). As such, it is understandable that coaches would shy away from emotional disclosures through fear that the expression of guilt could be used as some form of evidence by others that the coach was indeed liable and negligent. Conversely, for coaches such as Andrew, the possibility of legal action was viewed as the most appropriate way in which he might compensate an athlete for a perceived wrongdoing. Compensation in the context of traumatic events has been linked to the witnesses' attempts to restore a sense of justice (Hafer & Bègue, 2005). However, the use of self-punishment has been recognised as a guilt-regulating strategy employed by supposed transgressors when direct compensation to the injured individual is not possible. Such action is often considered a signal of remorse and desire for reparation that serves to restore the transgressor's relationship with the harmed individual and increases the potential for forgiveness (Nelissen, 2012).

Conclusion

The current study sought to provide some initial insights into the multifaceted development and regulation of guilt in coaches. The results indicated that guilt may be embodied and managed in different ways. In some instances, guilt is an immediate visceral response to a sport injury, whereas on other occasions guilt may develop through the coach's reflection upon the incident. With regard to the latter, imaginary past scenarios may portray the coach's actions as foreseeably causal to the injury and insufficiently justified. Interestingly, in cases where the injured athlete was portrayed by the coach in a particularly positive or negative light, the potential for guilt could be heightened or quashed, respectively. However, this positive relationship between guilt and a coach's physical and/or personal proximity with the injured athlete did not hold across all circumstances.

In attempting to regulate guilt, the coaches described how keeping their distance from the injured athlete could provide a transient respite from their experiences of guilt. However, the continued avoidance of the injured athlete was also understood as an increasingly guilt-provoking course of action in itself. As such, while making contact with the injured athlete could be a problematic encounter for the coach, it could, also be a guilt dissipating and healing experience. In a more contentious trajectory of regulating guilt, it was found that a coach could engage in reparative action such as requesting the injured athlete to make a legal claim of negligence against him or her.

The claim that coaches will inevitably experience and thus need to regulate guilt in the context of sport injury is intuitive when we consider the wider social context in which the process of sports coaching currently takes place. Hardman and Jones (2013) suggested that the moral and ethical worlds of sports coaches are increasingly defined from a deontological perspective that centres on the coach's duties and their sports participants' entitlements. This is perhaps well evidenced in the development of generic standards of practice or codes of conduct. The standard duty of care is perhaps one of the most notable obligations of the coaching role in sport across all levels of competition, whereby the coach is required to exercise care to prevent reasonably foreseeable harm in light of specific circumstances (James, 2013). As Sports Coach UK (2005) stated, individuals with good coaching practice are those who, "ensure that the environment is as safe as possible, taking into account and minimising possible risks" (p. 3). Importantly, McNamee (2011) insightfully critiques codes of practice that have come into being through the professionalization of sports coaching, stating that they "franchise 'blameability' [sic] and consequently 'punishability' [sic] to their respective organisations" (p. 25).

Compounding this situation, is the "nebulous and woolly" nature of the standard duty of care that sports coaches are expected to champion. In practice, this fails to offer any articulation as to when the occurrence of an injury unequivocally does not infer a breach in the coach's obligated conduct (Partington, 2014, p. 236). Importantly, we may be left with a situation where the mere presence of injury is seen to reflect a coach's failure to fulfil expectations and standards associated with his or her sporting role. This certainly represents an important avenue for future inquiry and on-going consideration.

Acknowledgements

Thank you to the participants who generously gave their time and personal stories.

Disclosure statement

No potential conflict of interest was reported by the authors.

References

Abgarov, A., Jeffery-Tosoni, S., Baker, J., & Fraser-Thomas, J. (2012). Understanding social support throughout the injury process among interuniversity swimmers. *Journal of Intercollegiate Sport, 5*, 213–229.

American Psychiatric Association. (1994). *Diagnostic and statistical manual of mental disorders* (4th ed.). Washington, DC: Author.

American Psychiatric Association. (2013). *Diagnostic and statistical manual of mental disorders* (5th ed.). Arlington, VA: Author.

Andrews, M. (2000). Introduction. In M. Andrews, S. D. Sclater, C. Squire, & A. Treacher (Eds.), *Lines of narrative* (pp. 77–80). London: Routledge.

Baumeister, R. F., Stillwell, A. M., & Heatherton, T. F. (1994). Guilt: an interpersonal approach. *Psychological Bulletin, 115*, 243–267.

Bianco, T. (2001). Social support and recovery from sport injury: Elite skiers share their experiences. *Research Quarterly for Exercise and Sport, 72*, 376–388.

Blum, A. (2008). Shame and guilt, misconceptions and controversies: A critical review of the literature. *Traumatology: An International Journal, 14*, 91–102.

Bovin, M. J., & Marx, B. P. (2001). The importance of the peritraumatic experience in defining traumatic stress. *Psychological Bulletin, 137*, 47–67.

Browne, K. C., Trim, R. S., Myers, U. S., & Norman, S. B. (2015). Trauma-related guilt: Conceptual development and relationship with posttraumatic stress and depressive symptoms. *Journal of Traumatic Stress, 28*, 134–141.

Carnì, S., Petrocchi, N., Del Miglio, C., Mancini, F., & Couyoumdjian, A. (2013). Intrapsychic and interpersonal guilt: A critical review of the recent literature. *Cognitive Processing, 14*, 333–346.

Cassidy, T., Jones, R., & Potrac, P. (2009). *Understanding sports coaching. The social, cultural, and pedagogical foundations of coaching practice* (2nd ed.). Abingdon: Routledge.

Corbillon, F., Crossman, J., & Jamieson, J. (2009). Injured athletes' perceptions of the social support provided by their coaches and teammates during rehabilitation. *Journal of Sport Behavior, 32*, 93–107.

Day, M. C. (2012). Coping with Trauma in Sport. In J. Thatcher, M. Jones, & D. Lavallee (Eds.), *Coping and emotion in sport* (2nd ed., pp. 62–78). London: Routledge.

Day, M., Bond, K., & Smith, B. (2013). Holding it together: Coping with vicarious trauma in sport. *Psychology of Sport and Exercise, 14*(1), 1–11.

Denzin, N. K., & Lincoln, Y. S. (2008). Introduction: The discipline and practice of qualitative research. In N. K. Denzin & Y. S. Lincoln (Eds.), *The landscape of qualitative research* (pp. 1–43). London: Sage.

Elliot, J. (2005). *Using narratives in social research: Qualitative and quantitative approaches.* London: Sage.

Friedman, M. J. (2013). Finalizing PTSD in DSM-5: Getting here from there and where to go next. *Journal of Traumatic Stress, 26*, 548–556.

Frisch, A., Seil, R., Urhausen, A., Croisier, J. L., Lair, M. L., & Theisen, D. (2009). Analysis of sex-specific injury patterns and risk factors in young high-level athletes. *Scandinavian Journal of Medicine & Science in Sports, 19*, 834–841.

Gabert-Quillen, C. A., Fallon, W., & Delahanty, D. L. (2011). PTSD after traumatic injury: An investigation of the impact of injury severity and peritraumatic moderators. *Journal of Health Psychology, 16*, 678–687.

Grindstaff, J. S., Wrisberg, C. A., & Ross, J. R. (2010). Collegiate athletes' experience of the meaning of sport injury: A phenomenological investigation. *Perspectives in Public Health, 130*, 127–135.

Hafer, C. L., & Bègue, L. (2005). Experimental research on just-world theory: Problems, developments, and future challenges. *Psychological Bulletin, 131*, 128–167.

Hardman, A., & Jones, C. (2013). Philosophy for coaches. In R. L. Jones & K. Kingston (Eds.), *An introduction to sports coaching: Connecting theory to practice* (pp. 99–111). Abingdon: Routledge.

Hathaway, L. M., Boals, A., & Banks, J. B. (2011). PTSD symptoms and dominant emotional response to a traumatic event: An examination of DSM-IV criterion A2. *Anxiety, Stress, & Coping, 23*, 119–126.

James, M. (2013). *Sports law* (2nd ed.). Basingstoke: Palgrave MacMillan.

Janoff-Bulman, R. (1992). *Shattered assumptions. Towards a new psychology of trauma.* New York, NY: The Free Press.

Joseph, S., & Linley, P. A. (2005). Positive adjustment to threatening events: An organismic valuing theory of growth through adversity. *Review of General Psychology, 9*, 262–280.

Knowles, Z., Borrie, A., & Telfer, H. (2005). Towards the reflective sports coach: Issues of context, education and application. *Ergonomics, 48*, 1711–1720.

Kramp, M. K. (2004). Exploring life and experience through narrative inquiry. In K. deMarrais, & S. D. Lapan (Eds.), *Foundations of research: Methods of inquiry in education and the social sciences* (pp. 103–121). Mahwah, NJ: Lawrence Erlbaum Associates.

Kubany, E. S., & Watson, S. B. (2003). Guilt: Elaboration of a multidimensional model. *The Psychological Record, 53*, 51–90.

Kubany, E. S., & Manke, F. P. (1995). Cognitive therapy for trauma-related guilt: Conceptual bases and treatment outlines. *Cognitive and Behavioral Practice, 2*, 27–61.

Lee, D. A., Scragg, P., & Turner, S. (2001). The role of shame and guilt in traumatic events: A clinical model of shame-based and guilt-based PTSD. *British Journal of Medical Psychology, 74*, 451–466.

Lerias, D., & Byrne, M. K. (2003). Vicarious traumatization: Symptoms and predictors. *Stress and Health, 19*, 129–138.

Lieblich, A., Tuval-Mashiach, R., & Zilber, T. (1998). *Narrative research: Reading, analysis, and interpretation.* London: Sage.

Lincoln, Y. S., Lynham, S. A., & Guba, E. G. (2011). Paradigmatic controversies, contradictions, and emerging confluences, revisited. In N. K. Denzin & Y. S. Lincoln (Eds.), *The SAGE handbook of qualitative research* (4th ed., pp. 97–128). London: Sage.

Mattila, V. M., Parkkari, J., Koivusilta, L., Kannus, P., & Rimpelä, A. (2009). Participation in sports clubs is a strong predictor of injury hospitalization: A prospective cohort study. *Scandinavian Journal of Medicine & Science in Sports, 19*, 267–273.

McNamee, M. (2011). Celebrating trust, virtues and rules in the ethical conduct of sports coaches. In A. R. Hardman & C. Jones (Eds.), *The ethics of sports coaching* (pp. 23–41). Abingdon: Routledge.

Nelissen, R. M. (2012). Guilt-induced self-punishment as a sign of remorse. *Social Psychological and Personality Science, 3*, 139–144.

Ozer, E. J., Best, S. R., Lipsey, T. L., & Weiss, D. S. (2008). Predictors of posttraumatic stress disorder and symptoms in adults: A meta-analysis. *Psychological Trauma: Theory, Research, Practice, and Policy*, S(1), 3–36.

Park, C. (2010). Making sense of the meaning literature: An integrative review of meaning making and its effects on adjustment to stressful life events. *Psychological Bulletin, 136*, 257–301.

Partington, N. (2014). Legal liability of coaches: A UK perspective. *The International Sports Law Journal, 14*, 232–241.

Polkinghorne, D. E. (1991). Narrative and self concept. *Journal of Narrative and Life History, 1*, 135–153.

Polkinghorne, D. E. (1995). Narrative configuration in qualitative analysis. In J. A. Hatch & R. Wisniewski (Eds.), *Life history and narrative* (pp. 5–23). London: The Falmer Press.

Potrac, P., Jones, R. L., Purdy, L., Nelson, L., & Marshall, P. (2013). Towards an emotional understanding of coaching: A suggested research agenda. In P. Potrac, W. Gilbert, & J. Denison (Eds.), *Routledge handbook of sport coaching* (pp. 235–246). London: Routledge.

Pugh, L. R., Taylor, P. J., & Berry, K. (2015). The role of guilt in the development of post-traumatic stress disorder: A systematic review. *Journal of Affective Disorders, 182*, 138–150.

Richardson, L., & St. Pierre, E. A. (2005). Writing: A method of inquiry. In N. K. Denzin & Y. S. Lincoln (Eds.), *The SAGE handbook of qualitative research* (3rd ed., pp. 959–978). London: Sage.

Riessman, C. K. (2008). *Narrative methods for the human sciences*. London: Sage.

Robbins, J. E., & Rosenfeld, L. B. (2001). Athletes' perceptions of social support provided by their head coach, assistant coach, and athletic trainer, pre-injury and during rehabilitation. *Journal of Sports Behavior, 24*, 277–297.

Simon, R. L. (2013) Coaching, compliance and the law. In R. L. Simon (Ed.), *The ethics of coaching sports. Moral, social and legal issues* (pp. 187–192). Boulder, CO: Westview Press.

Smith, B., & Sparkes, A. C. (2009). Narrative inquiry in sport and exercise psychology: What can it mean, and why might we do it? *Psychology of Sport and Exercise, 10*, 1–11.

Smith, B., Sparkes, A. C., & Caddick, N. (2014). Judging qualitative research. In L. Nelson, R. Groom, & P. Potrac (Eds.), *Research methods in sports coaching* (pp. 192–202). London: Routledge.

Sparkes, A. C., & Smith, B. (2014). *Qualitative research methods in sport, exercise and health: From process to product*. London: Routledge.

Sports Coach, UK. (2005). *Codes of practice for sports coaches*. Leeds: The National Coaching Foundation.

Squire, C. (2008). Experience-centred and culturally orientated approaches to narrative. In M. Andrews, C. Squire, & M. Tamboukou (Eds.), *Doing narrative research* (pp. 47–71). London: Sage.

Walker, N., Thatcher, J., & Lavallee, D. (2007). Review: Psychological responses to injury in competitive sport: A critical review. *The Journal of the Royal Society for the Promotion of Health, 127*, 174–180.

Wiese-Bjornstal, D. M. (2010). Psychology and socioculture affect injury risk, response, and recovery in high-intensity athletes: A consensus statement. *Scandinavian Journal of Medicine & Science in Sport, 20*, 103–111.

Willig, C. (2008). *Introducing qualitative research in psychology: Adventures in theory and method*. Buckingham: Open University Press.

Understanding coach burnout and underlying emotions: a narrative approach

Kylie McNeill, Natalie Durand-Bush and Pierre-Nicolas Lemyre

ABSTRACT

The purpose of this study was to investigate coaches' subjective experiences of burnout in order to shed light on the complex emotional nature of this syndrome. Five full-time paid coaches (two women and three men) experiencing burnout participated in an in-depth individual interview as part of a larger 13-week intervention study. A content analysis of the interview data resulted in the construction of five non-fictional short stories highlighting the emotions underlying the coaches' experiences of burnout. The coaches described a variety of emotions including anxiety, anger, apathy and dejection, which had negative implications upon their well-being and coaching practice. Emotions were linked to the three dimensions of burnout; that is, emotional exhaustion, depersonalisation and reduced personal accomplishment. Findings support calls for intervention research to help coaches manage their emotions and prevent burnout.

Introduction

Coaching athletes can be a gratifying and rewarding pursuit (Raedeke, 2004). Indeed, coaches report deriving various benefits from their role, such as forming bonds with their athletes, enjoying seeing their athletes succeed, and making a contribution to their sport and community (Frey, 2007; Lorimer, 2009). At the same time, however, the process of coaching is often fraught with ambiguity and uncertainty (Thompson, Potrac, & Jones, 2015), as coaches operate within complex and dynamic work environments (McLean & Mallet, 2012). Within such contentious contexts, coaches "experience a variety of strong emotions as they strive to navigate the challenges and opportunities of their dynamic sporting worlds" (Potrac, Jones, Purdy, Nelson, & Marshall, 2013, p. 236). Despite this, coaches are often portrayed in the literature as being "free of emotionality" when this is clearly not the case (Nelson et al., 2013). Potrac and colleagues (2013) highlight that emotions can be understood as physiological, psychological and social phenomena, and argue that to accurately depict coaches' reality and find ways to help them meet the demands of their profession, a greater understanding of the emotional nature of coaching is needed.

One increasingly prevalent topic in the coaching literature that is depicted by great variations in emotion is that of burnout. Burnout is a psychological syndrome resulting from exposure to chronic stressors, wherein individuals perceive that their demands exceed their resources over an extended period of time (Kelley, 1994). As such, burnout can be thought of as the end result of a prolonged inability to effectively cope with stress (Cresswell & Eklund, 2007), and as an indicator of ill-being among coaches (Bentzen, Lemyre, & Done Henttä, 2015). Given that coaches often face a myriad of technical, physical, organisational and psychological demands that are not always met with adequate resources (Thelwell, Weston, Greenlees, & Hutchings, 2008), it is perhaps not surprising that they have been described as a population susceptible to burnout (Raedeke & Kenttä, 2013).

Burnout is, however, more than a stress response. It is a complex, multidimensional syndrome characterised by three main features: (a) emotional exhaustion (i.e. the individual stress component), (b) depersonalisation (i.e. the interpersonal component, which reflects an emotional and cognitive distancing from one's work), and (c) reduced personal accomplishment (i.e. the self-evaluative component in which one perceives a lack of achievement at work) (Maslach, Schaufeli, & Leiter, 2001). For coaches experiencing burnout then, the syndrome represents an inherently emotional experience in which one can feel depleted, overextended, cynical, detached, diminished and devalued (Kelley, 1994; Raedeke & Kenttä, 2013).

It is important to note that burnout does not represent an event, but rather a process in which individuals anticipating a sense of meaning from their work alternatively face increasing disillusionment and diminishing motivation towards it (Raedeke & Kenttä, 2013). As such, the syndrome is marked by a gradual change in functioning (Bentzen et al., 2015) and is associated with a variety of affective (e.g. depressed mood), cognitive (e.g. concentration problems), behavioural (e.g. withdrawal), physical (e.g. chronic fatigue) and motivational (e.g. apathy) symptoms (Goodger, Gorely, Lavallee, & Harwood, 2007).

In the occupational context, burnout is linked to employee ill-health, absenteeism and turnover (Maslach et al., 2001). In the context of coaching, the impact of burnout extends to not only coaches' health and well-being, but also their practice and relationships with athletes (Goodger et al., 2007). For example, Price and Weiss (2000) found that high-school coaches who scored high on emotional exhaustion were perceived by their athletes as giving less training, instruction and social support, and as withdrawing from coach–athlete interactions. Similarly, Vealey, Armstrong, Comar, and Greenleaf (1998) found that collegiate coaches who scored high on emotional exhaustion and depersonalisation were perceived by their athletes to be less empathetic, more autocratic, and less effective in their communication.

Unfortunately, little research attention has focused on the experiences and consequences of burnout among coaches. Even fewer studies have addressed the emotional component of burnout in this population. The literature is also marked by a lack of qualitative studies on coach burnout in general (e.g. Goodger et al., 2007), and has been limited primarily to samples of part-time or recreational coaches (e.g. Raedeke & Kenttä, 2013). However, in a recent qualitative study of eight elite male Swedish soccer coaches experiencing high levels of exhaustion, Lundkvist, Gustafsson, Hjälm, and Hassmén (2013) proposed two profiles of burnout experience. Specifically, the *performance environment profile* was associated with having a central identity as a coach and external pressure emanating from the performance culture of soccer. Coaches within this profile experienced anger, bitterness and cynicism, as well as behavioural changes (e.g. became antisocial). The *life situation profile*, on the other hand, was associated with overload, issues at work, and an overall difficulty managing different life contexts (e.g. family, coaching and other employment). Coaches who fit this profile typically experienced loss of energy, depressed mood, and physical disturbances (e.g. illness or panic attacks) resulting from exhaustion (Lundkvist et al., 2013). Findings from this initial study then, help to shed light on the causes and symptoms of burnout and underscore the emotional nature of this experience for coaches.

While Lundkvist and colleagues (2013) were able to discern two profiles in their data, it is also widely acknowledged that burnout is an individualised experience (Schaufeli & Buunk, 2003). As such, it would appear worthwhile to examine burnout from an idiographic perspective in order to further explore individual coaches' experiences of burnout (Goodger et al., 2007) and the emotions underlying these experiences. Indeed, the value of such an approach lies in the provision of rich, in-depth accounts that capture variations and retain important contextual information (Gould, Tuffey, Udry, & Loehr, 1997). By capturing the coaches' unique and diverse experiences, idiographic research provides an opportunity to increase our understanding of burnout (Gould et al., 1997), emotions (Potrac et al., 2013) and the process of coaching in general (Potrac, Brewer, Jones, Armour, & Hoff, 2000).

The purpose of this study was to investigate coaches' subjective experiences of burnout, with an emphasis on their emotions. A narrative approach was used as it lends itself well to an idiographic exploration of this topic. This type of inquiry is grounded in the perspective that narratives, or stories, play a crucial role in both constructing and reflecting individuals' reality. Narratives thus, have the potential to illuminate participants' personal experiences, while revealing their temporal, emotional and contextual nature and the inherent complexity of these experiences (Jones, 2009; Smith, 2010; Smith & Sparkes, 2009). Narratives also preserve the subjective nature of participants' lifeworlds, while simultaneously recognising the larger discourses that inform and constrain how they make sense of those worlds (Carless & Douglas, 2011; Sparkes & Partington, 2003). Within the coaching literature specifically, narrative research has been advocated as a means to illustrate and directly share the meaningful lived experiences (Callary, Werthner, & Trudel, 2012; Jones, 2009) of coaches in order to enrich our understanding of the nuanced, complex nature of coaching practice (Jones, 2006). In keeping with this approach, five non-fictional short stories were constructed in order to present a rich account of the emotions underlying the coaches' lived experiences of burnout.

Method

Participant selection

This study was part of a larger intervention-based project carried out with coaches experiencing burnout. Following ethical approval from the university's research ethics board, quantitative screening data were collected from 260 Canadian coaches through an online survey. Using this screening data, participants were recruited for the intervention if they were experiencing moderate to high levels of burnout, currently working as full-time paid coaches, and could speak, read and write in English. Burnout was assessed in the online survey using the Maslach Burnout Inventory – Educator's Survey (MBI-ES; Maslach, Jackson, & Leiter, 1996), which was adapted for coaches in keeping with previous studies (e.g. Hjälm, Kenttä, Hassmén, & Gustafsson, 2007). Although the MBI-ES is not a diagnostic tool, it does allow for scores to be classified as low, moderate and high based on normative data (Raedeke & Kenttä, 2013). Since emotional exhaustion and depersonalisation are considered the key dimensions of burnout (Demerouti, Bakker, Friedhelm, & Schaufeli, 2001), coaches were included in the study if they scored moderate to high on both the emotional exhaustion and depersonalisation subscales of the MBI-ES.

Five coaches participated in the study. Specifically, the three male and two female coaches ranged in age from 26 to 37 years, and possessed an average of 13 years' worth of coaching experience. All five of the participants held full-time paid coaching positions, with no secondary employment. Two of the coaches were figure skating coaches, while the others coached tennis, swimming and athletics. One coach worked with provincial-level athletes, three coached national-level athletes and one worked with athletes competing at an international level. All five coaches were either married or in a long-term relationship, and one was a parent. Four of the coaches had post-secondary education.

Data collection

After providing informed consent, the five coaches were invited to participate in an individual interview with the first author, prior to their participation in the intervention. The data collected from this interview served to fulfil the aim of this study. The semi-structured interviews (Rubin & Rubin, 2005) lasted between 50 and 100 min each, and aimed to explore the coaches' lived experience of burnout, in addition to other topics relevant to the larger intervention study (e.g. emotions, stress, well-being, self-regulation).

With respect to burnout, the interview guide (Rubin & Rubin, 2005) included open-ended, experiential/emotional, temporal and contextual questions in the hopes of encouraging coaches to share their subjective experiences. Specifically, coaches were asked to reflect on the meaning of burnout (e.g. what does burnout mean to you?), how they experienced it (e.g. what does burnout feel like?), how they were currently feeling (e.g. how have you been feeling lately?) and the consequences of burnout for them (e.g. how has burnout influenced your coaching and your health?). Follow-up probing questions grounded in the coaches' own language were asked when needed (e.g. when you say "drowning", what does that feel like? Can you elaborate?). The digitally recorded interviews were transcribed verbatim and sent to each coach for member checking (Culver, Gilbert, & Sparkes, 2012).

Data analysis

The first and second authors analysed the qualitative data in keeping with the procedures used by Carless and Sparkes (2008). To begin, the first author did an initial reading of all the interview transcripts to become familiar with the data. She then reduced each coach's transcript to the content that was relevant to his or her experience of burnout and underlying emotions, before embarking on a further series of close readings. Next, she conducted a first-level content analysis to inductively identify broader themes (e.g. emotional exhaustion, apathy) associated with the units of analysis within each transcript. A separate document was subsequently created for each coach condensing these themes and supporting units of analysis; a text which represented a mental map of each coach's experiences and emotions (Carless & Sparkes, 2008).

Using these themes and units of analysis in each mental map, the first author then constructed non-fictional short stories to illustrate the coaches' subjective experience of burnout and to bring the underlying emotions to life. At this point, the second author read all of the stories with the purpose of ensuring coherence and comprehensiveness. After discussing the content, the two authors agreed to make revisions to the final composition and, as such, employed authorial presence (Carless & Sparkes, 2008). That is, while each story is comprised of 92–96% of the coaches' own words, the authors made minimal changes to the narratives to enhance flow, clarify the original context of the story and/or protect the anonymity of the coaches.

Through this analytical approach, the authors adopted the stance of a *storyteller* (Smith & Sparkes, 2009), electing to value the voices of Molly, Gordon, Brooke, Michael and Andy (all pseudonyms) by representing the data in the form of first-person narratives. Nonetheless, it is important to note that the stories are by their very nature co-constructions. Simply put, the authors created meaning when constructing the narratives and selecting which elements of the story they deemed important to *show* (Jones, Armour, & Potrac, 2003). Moreover, while recognising that writing and representation are forms of analysis in their own right (Sparkes, 2002), the authors offer interpretation through their reflections on the stories in the discussion section of the paper.

The authors also evoke the following questions upon which to reflect when evaluating the stories (Carless & Sparkes, 2008) since non-fictional narratives remain a novel form of representation in the sport psychology (Carless & Sparkes, 2008) and coaching (Callary et al., 2012) literature(s): Are these stories coherent and credible? Are they constructed in a manner that is comprehensible and meaningful? Are there moral and ethical considerations in the way the coaches are portrayed? Additionally, in light of the aim of the study, readers are encouraged to consider the following questions: Do the stories provide a rich account of the coaches' lived experiences of burnout? Are the emotions that underlie these experiences brought to life in these stories? Do these stories contribute to our understanding of coaches' subjective experiences of burnout and emotions in a significant way? And, do they inspire an interpretive response? Bearing these considerations in mind, Molly, Gordon, Brooke, Michael and Andy's non-fictional stories are presented.

Results

Mountains and crashes (Molly, figure skating)

The last six months have been basically hell. Really, really bad. I have been physically exhausted. I've been going in and giving the kids everything I have and then coming home and just crashing on the couch, either starving or not even able to smell food without being sick to my stomach. When I'm burned out, I get apathetic and look at the kid and say, "My god, you're probably not going to ever get to the next level of skating. What's the point, why are you here?" Like "I'm just an expensive babysitter for you" or "I'm just an ineffective personal trainer for you". And then it snowballs and it starts to creep into the work I do with the kids who really do want to be there and really do have the ability or the drive or the talent to be successful. And that's the worst thing, when I start turning into that, when I should be really into giving everything I have to those kids who have a shot at making it.

And it's harder to see the big picture when I'm angry or spun out or overstressed. I fixate on one thing at the expense of a well-rounded training session, or carry over that sense of apathy or detachment, and before I know it, a week's gone by and I've accomplished nothing. Or I feel like no matter what exercise I give the kids, it's the wrong one, and I lose faith in my abilities as a coach. I start questioning everything that I'm doing. And it's extreme, in one week I can touch on all these different places. It's never even, there's mountains and then crashes, and it's constant like this. And I hope that the kids don't pick on it, but they're not stupid. I'm sure they can tell when I'm having a bad day and I'm yelling at them to get their arms up and stretch their legs, or I'm telling them that they're not demonstrating appropriate work ethic for their level or goals. And I don't want to get to the point where I can't tell them the truth if they need to hear it, but sometimes I get too harsh and I get too negative, and it builds this atmosphere where nothing creative can happen.

I'm always an emotional person, but when my nerves are on edge it's much more so. I used to be very weepy, but now it's more "quick to anger". I'll snap at my students when I don't want to, I'll snap at my partner which I should never do, but I do. Or else I'm very apathetic. I feel nothing or I feel like nothing matters anyway so why bother trying? And I think if I didn't detach myself, then I would feel things negatively even more. So at least if I shut down or say, "Screw it, it doesn't matter anyway" then I don't have to feel those things.

But then it gets me to a certain point where I snap out of it and think "I'm not supposed to be this person, I'm supposed to be competitive, successful, high-achieving". So I'll throw myself into work and start the whole cycle again. And it's hard to turn work off; coaching *is* my daily life in the sense that it's difficult to separate. So when I get home and I want to relax, sometimes I can't because my thoughts keep spinning. And I know that I can't keep doing what I'm doing now for more than a few years and still be okay, but it seems like the one day that I do something for my well-being, I come back and all the cards have somehow fallen off my house. So I feel like I can only be safe, in terms of work, money, and everything, if I put myself last.

I can't escape the thoughts (Gordon, tennis)

There will be times when I don't want to coach because I'm burned out. Mentally I will tap out sometimes. Like right before Christmas I was absolutely zapped. I had nothing. It was really tough because all I wanted to do was just be done and go home for Christmas. And even when I came back, I resisted getting back into my routine. Even now, I don't want to eat well, I just want to eat junk food. I just want to drink; I want to come home and drink beer instead of going to bed early. But my burnout also ends up being psychological. I become obsessed with it, where I can't get the kid's serve or the fact that they aren't improving out of my head. It drains me physically and more than anything, it consumes my mind so much that it's like I've been asleep for eight hours but I haven't slept well because I've just had the same thought over and over again. So, on my day off, I didn't actually get a day off, because I spent the whole time with that serve in my mind and I don't feel refreshed. So when I'm burned out, I can't get away, I can't escape the thoughts.

Coaching is so wound into my existence, so that's the danger of it and how it can become draining. I try to guard how many hours of coaching per week I do. I try not to do more than three hours in a row because I try to be as engaged as I can be, so it can be very tiring. But any time I start feeling tired, it's almost always because I am in a rocky part in a relationship with someone or the hours I put in are spent mostly fighting and pushing hard. If I get frustrated, it's usually that I feel I am not doing a good enough job with the kids, or I feel like they're not doing enough, that I'm the one working harder than them. That really bothers me. I'm not going to give more emotionally than they're able to, and any time I have, it hasn't worked out very well. So I get run down because I don't get enough breaks, or the people I'm coaching are not the right people for me, and I don't feel I get enough out of the relationship.

The first thing I always notice is my shoulders clench up and they go really hard. And I have this feeling of anger, and sometimes I start to panic. I get anxiety where I'm trying to show them something and I'm doing it nervously, like "This has got to work". Or I'm jumping around because I'm starting to lose the purpose of the session and I can't focus myself enough to stay on one topic. Because I've had success very quickly with some kids, I have a belief that I can do it, so if it's not working right away, I tend to really get anxious. And it makes me really, really tough with the kids. I've found ways to make it so I'm not personalising things, but I can really call them out hard. So I have to be careful because I can do it in a way that's not the nicest. And while I put a huge amount of responsibility on them, if a kid doesn't make it, in the back of my head I'm thinking I just didn't work well enough, like I needed a different tool or something. And I have a hard time letting go of that.

All or nothing (Brooke, figure skating)

Burnout starts off with feeling overwhelmed, and then it turns into a disinterest in coaching. I don't feel like I'm doing as good of a job when I'm coaching. I start to feel like I need a break because I'm feeling run down. Like this past week I've felt overwhelmed. I feel like I'm being pulled in a couple different directions and I haven't been able to make a decision about how I'm going to handle some situations. And last night I was awful. I could even hear it in my voice with my skaters and I could tell from their response that I wasn't talking to them the way I normally would and I was trying to bring myself back, but I can't just call in sick. I can't just say, "This is a bad day". I have to go in. I have to push through it somehow. But I don't think I have good coping skills for dealing with high pressure situations. I don't know how to say no. So there's a lot of burnout that happens with me, and I don't cope well when that starts to happen.

Physically, I start getting sick. And it generally coincides with my skaters' peaks and valleys. So as my skaters are supposed to be peaking, I start getting sick. And it's been a pattern for eight years now, about five times throughout a year. I actually have anxiety attacks, I get pain in my chest and I get panicky, I get nervous and I have butterflies in my stomach. And I can't think clearly because I have too many things I'm thinking about. I've tried everything I can to make sure it doesn't happen, I've asked different people their strategies, but it just doesn't seem to work for me, because I want so much for my athletes. I feel like I owe them so much that it's hard for me to follow through with those plans or not feel guilty if I take time. I just feel really responsible for my athletes' outcomes. It almost feels like it's all or nothing. I'm going to give it all or I'm going to give it nothing at all. So I wish sometimes that I was less emotionally invested, because I think if I could be, I would be more effective and more consistent. But I also think that part of it is what makes me good at what I do.

And I'm a black-and-white thinker, so it's really hard for me when things start to falter to stay in the white so then I go in the black. And then I start to feel "oh forget it, I might as well stop doing this and try something different because this is killing me"; or "it's overwhelming and it's too much for me, so I'm just going to stop". But coaching *is* my life, I couldn't imagine doing anything else. Although I often say I want to quit, it is who I am. I'm a coach first, I'm a wife third, and I'm a mother second, a daughter last. So I do feel that my day is that. It's just hard because I'm in a bad place right now. I feel very unhealthy because I haven't had time this year to take care of myself the way I need to.

I'm drowning (Michael, swimming)

For the first three years, I was able to fulfil [my duties], "full steam ahead", no problem. Then we brought in the other swim team and I started to slow down. The next two or three years I felt like I was treading water, and last year and this year particularly, I've really started to feel like I'm drowning. It hasn't been as joy-filled as it used to be. It's been more of a labour than it has been. And I don't think it's the work, I think it's the circumstances. So I have to make the decision if I want to continue in those circumstances, recognising that I'm starting to throw good money after bad. Like, "when should I cut my losses?" But then the other question is, "What else do I do?" It's not that I don't have other marketable skills, but I haven't really done anything else. My whole entire life has been wrapped around a pool for 35 years, so "trapped" isn't probably the best word, but I can't really articulate it in another way.

It's a lot of mental exhaustion. It's emotional exhaustion too. When you're at a swim meet with 15, 20, 30 kids and you're watching each one of those 30 swimmers race four to six races, there's an emotional investment that happens as well. I feel the crash as a coach way more than I ever did as a swimmer, because I'm emotionally invested with everything that's happening. I don't have any downtime. I'm constantly on, constantly looking at performance, getting kids ready for the next one, getting kids off of their last one. Whether it was the highest of highs, or the lowest of lows, I'm getting them to focus on their next race. And coaches, we're the worst at taking our advice; we will worry 90,000 times more about one kid on the team than we're going to worry about ourselves. So that investment with 15, 20, 30 swimmers adds up. It gets pretty draining.

And it's not fun going to work knowing I used to like it. Like I used to really, really love what I do, and I know I had more energy, more passion, more excitement four years ago than I do today. And I feel there are days where I'm apathetic, and even though ten years ago I swore up and down, looking at old coach after old coach after old coach that I would never be that guy, I'm starting to be that guy. That's not enjoyable from a professional or a personal standpoint, especially when I look at it from the context of what is the experience or quality that I'm supplying to the athletes. Where I used to be more understanding and take the longer road with some of them, I'm less likely to do that now. I'm not going to go three to their one for us to make four. If they're going to invest themselves in what we're doing, then I'll invest equally. At the end of the day though, I don't want their legacy of swimming to have been, "That jackass swim coach, all he did was train me to death and never bothered to talk to me as a person". I don't want that, and I also don't want them to get injured or burned out or anything else.

But it's hard to be energetic and fun in a personal relationship, whether it's my wife or whoever, when I'm tired and cynical. There have been days when I've come home and I know I've taken it out on my wife, just through being short-tempered or being disconnected. Then emotionally, I don't think I'm clinically depressed, I just know I'm not happy. But I know why I'm not happy and that's what makes it difficult. It's the chicken or the egg where I'm waiting for things at work to get better so I'm happy, but I'm not really happy and things are not getting better, so what do I do?

Going from 0 to 100 (Andy, track)

My first year I was employed, I was the head coach of Club X, and burnout would be a very good way to describe it. It was objectively a highly successful year for the club, for budgets, athletes, national teams, records, medals. Everything was amazing. Administratively though, it crushed me because I took on everything. It was a feeling of uncontrollable, continuous, consistent white noise in the brain. I couldn't turn the brain off, I couldn't detach, and it just turned into a downward cycle of continuing levels of stress. It wasn't physical pain, but physiological discomfort, like the body wasn't right and it was the psychological manifestations of that. I drank a few more beers every week, I didn't sleep well, I put on almost 20 lb of garbage weight. And when the club told me they wouldn't match the salary I was at, and I knew that my career at that moment was done, I was very happy to be done coaching. And for a good year, I didn't know if I was ever going to come back.

But coaching ultimately was where I wanted to be, it's just who I am. And when I coach, I go 0 to 100, I empty the gas tank. I go until there's nothing left and I'm on empty, and then if I need to take a morning to just check out, I do it. But that is hopefully every month or two months, rather than every week. I don't want to say "helplessness", but I just get a feeling that the world is crashing and if I don't recharge, I can't do anything about it. Like if I'm going to be successful and even if I'm going to be able to have a practice later, I need to go home and have a nap. So, yeah, burnout is something I'm aware of, it's always on my mind.

The large portion of my stress comes down to the number of roles I have. I wear three major hats, sometimes four or five or six, depending on the weekend. So if I'm at a track meet and I'm literally trying to wear all six of those hats at the same time, that means there's six different groups of people at a time who need my attention. So it feels a lot like I'm juggling. But I'm pretty good at sheltering. I take the viewpoint of "they don't need to know". My athletes have a job to do and when they show up at the track, I expect them to leave their stress, their lives, their parents, their dates, their jobs, and give me two, three, four hours of focus and time that they need to achieve their goals. So I don't want to be a negative part of that and I demand the same from myself. But my girlfriend might say that I can get a bit closed in. I don't see it as much, it's more, "I don't need to talk about it; I'm good".

Do I think I can continue this pace forever? Definitely not, but right now I have age and health and a bunch of things on my side. So I'm going to grind it out and do everything I can to be successful for myself and also hopefully lead that into my athletes' programmes and careers. If I'm going to be successful and my athletes are going to be successful, I need to make those sacrifices. There's a lot of things for which I want to be recognised and I guess the time is now when I need to put in the work. If I wanted to be a recreational coach, I'd find a different job and coach 6 h a week, but this is what I signed up to do.

Discussion

By adopting the approach of a *storyteller* and presenting the findings as stories, the authors invite readers to become co-constructors of knowledge through their own interpretations of the narratives based on their unique vantage points (Smith & Sparkes, 2009). For instance, coaches may see themselves within elements of these stories, while coach educators might reflect on the ways in which they prepare coaches to effectively manage the demands associated with their roles. Although the authors have chosen to *show* rather than *tell* stories (Smith & Sparkes, 2009), in this section they have opted to share their reflections on these stories and their contribution to our understanding of the emotions underlying coaches' subjective experiences of burnout.

The short stories presented reveal the personal and complex nature of burnout (Schaufeli & Buunk, 2003); the coaches' experiences were highly individualised and the emotions underlying these experiences also varied. For Molly, burnout manifested itself in feelings of apathy, cynicism, incompetence, anger and subsequent guilt over feeling this way (i.e. "I'm not supposed to be this person").

Gordon's experience was characterised by feelings of anger as well, but also by frustration, anxiety and doubt (i.e. "I just didn't work well enough"). In Brooke's case, burnout was associated with anxiety, in addition to guilt, incompetence and dejection (i.e. "I'm in a bad place right now"). Michael also expressed dejection (i.e. "I don't think I'm clinically depressed, I just know I'm not happy"), and further described feelings of apathy, cynicism and disillusionment. Finally, Andy felt helpless and distressed in association with his experience of burnout (e.g. "It just turned into a downward cycle of continuing levels of stress"). The range of emotions described by the coaches, including anxiety, anger, frustration, apathy, cynicism and dejection, mirror those reported by athletes (e.g. Cresswell & Eklund, 2006; Gould, Tuffey, Udry, & Loehr, 1996; Gustafsson, Kenttä, Hassmén, Lundqvist, & Durand-Bush, 2008) and coaches (Lundkvist et al., 2013), and speak to the affective nature of this syndrome in general (Shirom, 2003).

Although the coaches' experiences were individualised, a salient emotional aspect underlying all of their encounters with burnout was a sense of depletion, reflecting the emotional exhaustion dimension of the syndrome. This is perhaps not surprising if one considers that emotional exhaustion is the defining feature of burnout (Maslach et al., 2001; Shirom, 2003). Congruent with the findings of Lundkvist and colleagues' (2013) study, the coaches experienced exhaustion physically, through sleep disturbances, fatigue, loss of energy and physiological discomfort (e.g. Andy's experience of "uncontrollable, continuous, consistent white noise in the brain"). However, their exhaustion was also emotional in nature, as the coaches described feeling drained, tapped out, run down, zapped and "on empty". Reflecting the stress response associated with emotional exhaustion (Maslach et al., 2001), Brooke felt overwhelmed and as if she was "being pulled in a couple different directions", while Molly described feeling overstressed, spun out, and "on edge". For Andy, emotional exhaustion was associated with feelings of helplessness: "I just get a feeling that the world is crashing and if I don't recharge, I can't do anything about it".

Another emotional aspect of the coaches' subjective experiences of burnout was that of depersonalisation, which featured in four of the five coaches' narratives through feelings of cynicism, apathy and disillusionment. Interestingly, Molly described a form of cognitive and emotional distancing most akin to depersonalisation through a negative, indifferent attitude towards her athletes (i.e. "My god, you're probably not going to ever get to the next level of skating. What's the point, why are you here?") enacted as a coping response in the face of growing exhaustion (Raedeke & Kenttä, 2013). In contrast, Brooke expressed a disinterest in coaching, while Michael felt apathetic, cynical and disillusioned about his job (i.e. asking himself, "when should I cut my losses?"). However, neither described these feelings in relation to their athletes. These experiences might be more aptly seen as a devaluation of their coaching, similar to the dimension of sport devaluation exhibited in athletic burnout (Raedeke & Smith, 2009). Indeed, Gordon expressed a form of emotional withdrawal from coaching through his desire to "just be done and go home for Christmas", which parallels symptoms of sport devaluation experienced by rugby players in Cresswell and Eklund's (2006) study (e.g. thinking about the end of the season, looking forward to the holidays). Researchers may want to further investigate the salience of the dimension of depersonalisation among coaches, as it has been argued that devaluation may be a better fit in this context (Lundkvist, Stenling, Gustafsson, & Hassmén, 2014).

Reduced personal accomplishment was also manifested emotionally through feelings of incompetence and doubt in three of the coaches' stories. For instance, Brooke expressed feelings of incompetence (e.g. "I don't feel like I'm doing as good of a job when I'm coaching"), while Molly described losing faith in her abilities as a coach and a lack of achievement, which she attributed to her feelings of apathy (e.g. "before I know it, a week's gone by and I've accomplished nothing"). Gordon also alluded to a sense of inefficacy and doubt (e.g. "in the back of my head I'm thinking I just didn't work well enough, like I needed a different tool"), which subsequently led to feelings of anxiety and frustration in terms of not "doing a good enough job with the kids". In this way, these coaches' stories speak to the self-evaluative aspect of burnout and the difficulty of achieving a sense of accomplishment when one is emotionally exhausted and/or devaluing his or her work (Maslach et al., 2001).

In addition to feelings of incompetence and a perceived lack of achievement, the stories also shed light on the impact burnout had on their coaching behaviours. Specifically, reflecting the physiological and social nature of emotions in general (Potrac et al., 2013), the coaches described how their negative emotions were embodied and embedded socially within the interpersonal context of coaching. For instance, Brooke's feeling of being overwhelmed was embodied through an "awful" tone of voice, while Gordon's frustration was manifested socially through "fighting and pushing hard" and being "really, really tough" on his athletes. Molly's anger also led to her being "too harsh" and yelling and snapping at her skaters, while Michael's dejection and apathy resulted in him being less tolerant and understanding of his athletes. Taken together, these findings lend additional support to earlier studies suggesting that coach burnout may have negative implications for athletes (Price & Weiss, 2000; Vealey et al., 1998).

Moreover, these four coaches expressed concern regarding how their emotional manifestations of burnout were potentially negatively influencing the quality of their athletes' sporting experiences. For example, Molly acknowledged that the kids can tell when she's having a bad day, and Michael worried about developing the legacy of being a "jackass swim coach". These concerns suggest an awareness of a discrepancy between what these coaches were feeling and expressing to their athletes and what they believed they *should* feel and express during the social exchange of coaching (Hochschild, 1979). Hochschild's (1979, 1983) work on emotional labour and emotion management provides a useful theoretical lens through which to examine these "feeling rules" (i.e. the socially shared rules that guide how one ought to feel in a particular context; Hochschild, 1979) and question the socialisation process through which coaches internalise the norms around emotional expression (Potrac et al., 2013). For instance, in contrast to the other four coaches, Andy described "sheltering" his athletes from his emotions, stating "I don't want to be a negative part of that and I demand the same from myself". This is indicative of Andy's engagement in "surface acting" with his athletes, where he consciously changed his outward expression to meet the "display rules" (i.e. the rules that govern when and how overt emotional expressions occur in specific situations; Hochschild, 1979) he felt necessary to comply with (Nelson et al., 2013). As such, it may speak to how Andy felt constrained by larger discourses surrounding norms for emotional management in coaching (Potrac et al., 2013), thus providing additional context to his experience of burnout.

Although only Andy explicitly described engaging in "surface acting" to purposefully manage or conceal how he felt, all five coaches' stories highlight the intense personal and emotional "investment of the self in practice" (Potrac et al., 2013, p. 238) and reveal how this investment contributed to their sense of depletion and burnout. For instance, Gordon described needing to limit his coaching hours in order to be "as engaged as possible", while Michael explained how being "constantly on" with his athletes was draining. Moreover, Brooke and Molly's stories revealed how giving their athletes "all or nothing" (Brooke) and "everything" (Molly) characterised their subjective experiences of burnout. At a more implicit level, these findings allude to the emotion work and emotional stamina (Hochschild, 1983) that may be required to successfully perform as a coach.

Interestingly, Hochschild (1983) contended that prolonged emotion management could lead to important psychological costs, including burnout. In line with this, Nelson and colleagues (2013) found that engaging in emotion management could negatively impact a coach's motivation and enthusiasm for his job. As such, it would also be valuable to examine in future studies how burnout may affect coaches' ability to engage in the emotion work needed to meet the feeling and display rules (Hochschild, 1979) associated with their practice. For example, Brooke described an inability to bring herself back when she sensed her voice was "awful" due to her depleted state, and Molly expressed how she snapped at her athletes even though she "didn't want to". In this way, the coaches' narratives point to the need for coaches to be able to not only recognise discrepancies between how they are feeling and how they want to feel (Hochschild, 1979), but also to enact self-regulation strategies to bring themselves in line with their preferred standards (Zimmerman, 2000), even when their personal resources are depleted (Durand-Bush, Collins, & McNeill, 2012).

This argument is particularly important, given that the narratives revealed negative implications of burnout for the coaches themselves. For instance, in addition to adverse consequences for the coaches' physical health (e.g. panic attacks, illness, sleep disturbances, weight gain, drinking, resistance to exercise and healthy eating), burnout depleted their emotional well-being. Michael's narrative in particular described a loss of motivation, enjoyment and passion for coaching, a role he had previously enjoyed, which was associated with feeling trapped, unhappy and dejected, a state he defined as "drowning". Molly's experience of "mountains and crashes" demonstrate that it may be difficult to sustain coaching due to fluctuations in emotional well-being (i.e. "I couldn't keep doing what I'm doing now for more than a few years and still be okay. It seems like the one day I do something for my well-being, I come back and all the cards have somehow fallen off my house"). Ultimately, three of the five coaches alluded to leaving coaching, whilst one coach left the profession but eventually returned, suggesting that burnout may have implications for coach retention (Raedeke & Manttä, 2013).

Conclusion

In conclusion, this study sheds light on a variety of strong emotions involved in coaching from the perspective of those experiencing burnout, and in so doing, provided a more human and vulnerable account of coaching practice (Potrac et al., 2013). Using a narrative approach to depict the emotions underlying coaches' experiences of burnout provides a novel feature, and while the aim was not to generalise findings to all coaches, readers are able to draw meaningful interpretations from the stories presented. Nonetheless, it is important to note that the sample was limited to five full-time, paid individual sport coaches, while the stories were co-constructed by us as authors. Future research could include coaches from other contexts (e.g. team sports, part-time or voluntary) and build on the findings from this study to further increase our understanding of the emotional nature of coach burnout. As one of the few qualitative studies on coach burnout, however, this investigation provided an in-depth account of depleted states experienced by coaches and their negative impact on coaches' well-being and practice. In this way, these stories speak further to the need for interventions to assist coaches in effectively regulating their emotions and behaviours in order to prevent or manage burnout and achieve optimal well-being in spite of the demands they face (Durand-Bush et al., 2012). Finally, readers are also encouraged to consider the use of narratives as a relevant pedagogical tool in coach education to promote reflection (Douglas & Carless, 2008) on emotions and burnout, and to further nurture self-regulation and well-being (Durand-Bush et al., 2012).

Acknowledgements

The authors would like to thank Molly, Gordon, Brooke, Michael and Andy for sharing their stories with us.

Disclosure statement

No potential conflict of interest was reported by the authors.

Funding

This work was supported by the Social Sciences and Humanities Research Council of Canada under a Joseph-Bombardier Canada Graduate Scholarship [grant number 767-2011-1253]; and the Ontario Ministry of Training, Colleges and Universities under an Ontario Graduate Scholarship.

References

Bentzen, M., Lemyre, P.-N., & Kenttä, G. (2015). The process of burnout among professional sport coaches through the lens of self-determination theory: A qualitative approach, *Sports Coaching Review, 3*, 101–116.

Callary, B., Werthner, P., & Trudel, P. (2012). How meaningful episodic experiences influence the process of becoming an experienced coach. *Qualitative Research in Sport, Exercise and Health, 4*, 420–438.

Carless, D., & Douglas, K. (2011). Stories as personal coaching philosophy. *International Journal of Sports Sciences & Coaching, 6*(1), 1–12.

Carless, D., & Sparkes, A. C. (2008). The physical activity experiences of men with serious mental illness: Three short stories. *Psychology of Sport and Exercise, 9*, 191–210.

Cresswell, S. L., & Eklund, R. C. (2006). The nature of player burnout in rugby: Key characteristics and attributions. *Journal of Applied Sport Psychology, 18*, 219–239.

Cresswell, S. L., & Eklund, R. C. (2007). Athlete burnout and organizational culture: An English rugby replication. *International Journal of Sport Psychology, 38*, 365–387.

Culver, D. M., Gilbert, W., & Sparkes, A. (2012). Qualitative research in sport psychology journals: The next decade 2000–2009 and beyond. *The Sport Psychologist, 26*, 261–281.

Demerouti, E., Bakker, A. B., Nachreiner, F., & Schaufeli, W. B. (2001). The job demands-resources model of burnout. *Journal of Applied Psychology, 86*, 499–512.

Douglas, K., & Carless, D. (2008). Using stories in coach education. *International Journal of Sports Science and Coaching, 3*, 33–49.

Durand-Bush, N., Collins, J., & McNeill, K. (2012). Women coaches' experiences of stress and self-regulation: A multiple case study. *International Journal of Coaching Science, 6*, 21–43.

Frey, M. (2007). College coaches' experiences with stress: "Problem solvers have problems, too". *The Sport Psychologist, 21*, 38–57.

Goodger, K., Gorely, T., Lavallee, D., & Harwood, C. (2007). Burnout in sport: A systematic review. *The Sport Psychologist, 21*, 127–151.

Gould, D., Tuffey, S., Udry, E., & Loehr, J. (1996). Burnout in competitive junior tennis players: II. Qualitative analysis. *The Sport Psychologist, 10*, 341–366.

Gould, D., Tuffey, S., Udry, E., & Loehr, J. (1997). Burnout in competitive junior tennis players: III. Individual differences in the burnout experience. *The Sport Psychologist, 11*, 257–276.

Gustafsson, H., Kenttä, G., Hassmén Lundqvist, C., & Durand-Bush, N. (2008). The process of burnout: A multiple case study of three elite endurance athletes. *International Journal of Sport Psychology, 38*, 388–416.

Hjälm, S., Kenttä, G., Hassmén, P., & Gustafsson, H. (2007). Burnout among elite soccer coaches. *Journal of Sport Behavior, 30*, 415–427.

Hochschild, A. R. (1979). Emotion work, feeling rules, and social structure. *American Journal of Sociology, 85*, 551–575.

Hochschild, A. R. (1983). *The managed heart: Commercialization of human feeling*. Berkeley, CA: University of California Press.

Jones, R. (2006). Dilemmas, maintaining "face", and paranoia: An average coaching life. *Qualitative Inquiry, 12*, 1012–1021.

Jones, R. L. (2009). Coaching as caring (the smiling gallery): Accessing hidden knowledge. *Physical Education and Sport Pedagogy, 14*, 377–390.

Jones, R. L., Armour, K. M., & Potrac, P. (2003). Constructing expert knowledge: A case study of a top-level professional soccer coach. *Sport, Education and Society, 8*, 213–229.

Kelley, B. C. (1994). A model of stress and burnout in collegiate coaches: Effects of gender and time of season. *Research Quarterly for Exercise and Sport, 65*, 48–58.

Lorimer, R. (2009). Coaches' satisfaction with their athletic partnerships. *International Journal of Coaching Science, 3*, 57–66.

Lundkvist, E., Gustafsson, H., Hjälm, S., & Hassmén, P. (2013). An interpretative phenomenological analysis of burnout and recovery in elite soccer coaches. *Qualitative Research in Sport, Exercise and Health, 4*, 400–419.

Lundkvist, E., Stenling, A., Gustafsson, H., & Hassmén, P. (2014). How to measure coach burnout: An evaluation of three burnout measures. *Measurement in Physical Education and Exercise Science, 18*, 209–226.

Maslach, C., Jackson, S. E., & Leiter, M. P. (1996). *Maslach burnout inventory manual* (3rd ed.). Palo Alto, CA: Consulting Psychologists Press.

Maslach, C., Schaufeli, W. B., & Leiter, M. P. (2001). Job burnout. *Annual Review of Psychology, 52*, 397–422.

McLean, K. N., & Mallett, C. J. (2012). What motivates the motivators? An examination of sports coaches. *Physical Education & Sport Pedagogy, 17*, 21–35.

Nelson, L., Allanson, A., Potrac, P., Gale, L., Gilbourne, D., & Marshall, P. (2013). Thinking, feeling, acting: The case of a semi-professional soccer coach. *Sociology of Sport Journal, 30*, 467–486.

Potrac, P., Brewer, C., Jones, R., Armour, K., & Hoff, J. (2000). Toward an holisticunderstanding of the coaching process. *Quest, 52*, 186–199.

Potrac, P., Jones, R. L., Purdy, L., Nelson, L., & Marshall, P. (2013). Towards an emotional understanding of coaching practice: A suggested research agenda. In P. Potrac, W. Gilbert, & J. Denison (Eds.), *Routledge handbook of sports coaching* (pp. 235–245). Florence, KY: Routledge.

Price, M. S., & Weiss, M. R. (2000). Relationships among coach burnout, coach behaviors, and athletes' psychological responses. *The Sport Psychologist, 14*, 391–401.

Raedeke, T. D. (2004). Coach commitment and burnout: A one-year follow-up. *Journal of Applied Sport Psychology, 16*, 333–349.

Raedeke, T. D., & Kenttä, G. (2013). Coach burnout. In P. Potrac, W. Gilbert, & J. Denison (Eds.), *Routledge handbook of sports coaching* (pp. 424–435). Florence, KY: Routledge.

Raedeke, T. D., & Smith, A. L. (2009). *The athlete burnout questionnaire manual*. Morgantown, WV: Fitness Information Technology.

Rubin, H. J., & Rubin, I. S. (2005). *Qualitative interviewing: The art of hearing data* (2nd ed.). Thousand Oaks, CA: Sage.

Schaufeli, W. B., & Buunk, B. P. (2003). Burnout: An overview of 25 years of research and theorizing. In M. J. Schabracq, J. A. Winnubst, & C. L. Cooper (Eds.), *Handbook of work and health psychology* (pp. 383–425). Chichester: Wiley.

Shirom, A. (2003). Job-related burnout: A review. In J. C. Quick, & L. E. Tetrick (Eds.), *Handbook of occupational health psychology* (pp. 245–264). Washington, DC: American Psychological Association.

Smith, B. (2010). Narrative inquiry: ongoing conversations and questions for sport and exercise psychology research. *International Review of Sport and Exercise Psychology, 3*, 87–107.

Smith, B., & Sparkes, A. C. (2009). Narrative analysis and sport and exercise psychology: Understanding lives in diverse ways. *Psychology of Sport and Exercise, 10*, 279–288.

Sparkes, A. C. (2002). *Telling tales in sport and physical activity: A qualitative journey*. Champaign, IL: Human Kinetics.

Sparkes, A. C., & Partington, S. (2003). Narrative practice and its potential contribution to sport psychology: The example of flow. *The Sport Psychologist, 17*, 292–317.

Thelwell, R. C., Weston, N. J. V., Greenlees, I. A., & Hutchings, N. V. (2008). Stressors in elite sport: A coach perspective. *Journal of Sports Sciences, 26*, 905–918.

Thompson, A., Potrac, P., & Jones, R. (2015). 'I found out the hard way': Micro-political workings in professional football. *Sport, Education and Society, 20*, 976–994.

Vealey, R., Armstrong, L., & Comar, W. (1998). Influence of perceived coaching behaviors on burnout and competitive anxiety in female college athletes. *Journal of Applied Sport Psychology, 10*, 297–318.

Zimmerman, B. J. (2000). Attaining self-regulation: A social-cognitive perspective. In M. Boekaerts, P. R. Pintrich, & M. Zeidner (Eds.), *Handbook of self-regulation* (pp. 13–42). San Diego, CA: Academic Press.

My eyes got a bit watery there: using stories to explore emotions in coaching research and practice for injured, sick and wounded military personnel

Kitrina Douglas and David Carless

ABSTRACT

Recognising the importance of holistic approaches to sport coaching pedagogy, there has been a move to include and understand more fully emotional and subjective features of coaches' work. Our research here seeks to advocate for and support this pedagogy. Ethnographic data were collected at a golf intervention where civilian sport coaches worked among serving injured, sick and wounded military personnel in a recovery context. We adopted a storytelling methodology to render present aspects of sport coaching that have previously been absent, particularly those of emotional and empathic understanding. This form of analysis and representation allowed multiple, dialogic meanings to evolve and a more sophisticated understanding of the role and contribution of the coach/leader in this unusual disability sport context. Through a series of vignettes which represented different aspects of the intervention, light is shed on how emotions are evoked, hidden or made visible depending on different situations and relationships. The stories also show some of the potential costs or risks of becoming more empathic and caring. Feedback from the coaches and programme participants suggested the stories illuminated some aspects of their lives, work and relationships that remain difficult to articulate and share.

Preface

It is generally recognised that we need to include, within our field of reference, human subjectivities – particularly feelings and emotions. Indeed, emotions play a leading role in interpersonal relationships (Dallos, 2006), and have been described as messengers from the self that provide a medium to interpret and respond to one's own and other people's actions, behaviours and experiences (Hochschild, 1983/2003). If we accept that effective coaching has at its heart an effective relationship (Côté & Gilbert, 2009; Jowett, 2005; Lyle, 1999; Wang, 2013), then we must also accept that in any given coaching scenario, we have a 'thinking, feeling, human being' interacting with other 'thinking, feeling, human beings' and emotions will be 'at work'. Yet emotional dimensions of sport coaching have often been marginalised or even absent from sports coaching research and educational provision (Potrac, Jones, Purdy, Nelson, & Marshall, 2013). Recognising the importance of holistic approaches, there has been a move recently to incorporate emotional knowledge in sport coaching and physical activity pedagogy (Douglas & Carless, 2008; Jones & Turner, 2006; Morgan, Jones, Gilbourne, & Llewellyn, 2012). Our research here seeks to advocate for and support this pedagogy.

Antoine (1996) and DePauw (1990) have suggested disability sport coaching requires a coach to develop a greater awareness of human subjectivities and emotions as each individual brings a somewhat unique challenge. Yet, as noted by DePauw and Gavron (2005), there is a lack of specialist education within disability sport. Our experience in mental health and coach education illustrates this lack of awareness (see Carless & Douglas, 2010). Seldom had the coaches we worked with considered how stigma and discrimination might have influenced their own emotional responses to an individual diagnosed with a mental: 'illness'. Indeed, it seemed many coaches were only aware of public stereotypes of, for example, 'a schizophrenic'. It was not unusual for coaches to be fearful of such individuals while also showing a lack of understanding for their lives. Along with DePauw and Gavron (2005), we support moves for more specialised education, and especially with novice and inexperienced coaches, before they enter disability sport coaching environments, which brings us to our current research.

Sport coaching among injured, sick and wounded military personnel

For several years, we have been researching a successful intervention named 'Battle Back, Lilleshall' aimed at supporting the recovery of wounded, injured and sick military personnel (e.g. Carless, 2014; Carless, Peacock, McKenna, & Cooke, 2013; Douglas & Carless, 2015a). The belief that sport can support recovery from physical and psychological injuries among military personnel is not new, and numerous types of activities have been used; for example, community fitness classes, mountaineering, surfing, fly-fishing, yoga. These activities are not an exhaustive list, but rather, provide examples of projects where a skilled practitioner provided specialist sport coaching and leadership.

It would seem reasonable to assume that delivering a rural monthly community exercise programme places different demands *on* and different considerations *for* a course leader/coach compared with a nine-day mountain expedition. Yet, to date, little attention has been devoted to understanding the unique challenges of coaching in these contexts. Despite research indicating that coaches and leaders are highly valued, that unique relationships are established, and that the coach was an integral part of the intervention (e.g. Carless et al., 2013), we know very little about the men and women behind delivery, their philosophies, motives or education. Nor have we accrued knowledge about the emotional demands this type of work brings. For example, there has been a paucity of research addressing the emotional costs or potential risks to individuals engaged in such roles. Such a state raises a number of concerns. What type of emotional demands surface when coaching wounded, injured or sick military personnel? How might we better prepare or support novice and/or inexperienced coaches? And how do those who fund such programmes justify and recognise the unique contribution of civilian coaches? One way to answer these questions is through stories.

Storytelling methodology

Qualitative researchers in sport and physical activity have found that traditional research methods are not well suited to exploring and or representing emotional connection, empathic understanding or embodied experience (Carless, 2012; Douglas, 2012, 2014a; McGannon, 2012). Indeed, Midgley (2001, p. 83) has observed that 'scientific concepts are not adapted to focusing on subjectivities', and that 'many of them have been carefully adapted to exclude it'. We have thus been challenged to find ways to preserve the multiplicity of human feeling we experience or witness through field research, and to communicate it without diminishing, devaluing or diluting its complexity or impact.

For us, a storytelling methodology sits within a broader narrative framework that recognises and values the creation and sharing of stories. For numerous authors (e.g. Frank, 2010; McLeod, 1997; Nelson, 2001), stories provide a way to make sense of our own and each other's experience, to give meaning and coherence to life's events and shape our sense of identity and self. It is not our intention here to advocate for all the potential contributions stories and storytelling within a narrative theoretical approach. That said, there are three issues that we would like to draw out.

Firstly, stories make it possible to convey emotionally significant information (Bruner, 1990). This is important in terms of understanding the demands civilian coaches face working in a military recovery context. Stories used in this way have the potential to take the reader into unfamiliar scenes, scenarios, relationships or issues with the characters in order to feel and experience *with* him or her, what is emotionally significant and why, as well as what is familiar and/or what might be unusual about this setting. If done well, the reader brings her own life experiences and interest to bear, broadening and extending her own horizons, as she gains a view of life from a different standpoint to her own. It is from such consideration that storied accounts have the potential to develop ethical and moral reflection (Frank, 2010), and to extend our awareness of emotional dimensions of coaching sport.

Secondly, sport is dominated by a hegemonically masculine type of story (Anderson, 2005), and a performance narrative (Douglas & Carless, 2015b) where winning is the most highly prized outcome and being tough, strong and powerful are highly valued assets. If stories about emotional engagement, loss, weakness, shame, empathic awareness or sensitivity do surface, they are often subsequently silenced, hidden, devalued and/or rendered taboo. One consequence is the dearth of stories to validate alternative ways of living and being in sport. Frank (2004) expands on this point, suggesting that,

> Stories do not merely narrate events. They convey on action and actor – either one or both – the socially accredited status of being worth notice. To render narratable is to claim relevance for action, and for the life of which that action is part. (p. 62)

In short, our lives only gain the status of 'being worthy' when they are noticed and valued by others. Without social accreditation, our actions become 'as if' they were invisible and worthless. Narrative research among high-performance athletes (e.g. Douglas, 2009, 2014b; Douglas & Carless, 2015b) has shown that, for some athletes, relationships, care and connection are more important than winning. Amplifying these stories challenges the performance narrative, a narrative plot where there is but 'one way' to 'be' or to 'find success' in sport. Dialogical storytelling, therefore, has an important role to play by rendering present what would otherwise be absent in coaching pedagogy, through validating the actions and stories of those who live with alternative values or whose actions go unnoticed.

A final ethical and moral benefit is that stories have the potential to remove artificial boundaries that research often creates between participants and the researcher. A storytelling methodology can be an effective way to preserve and reveal the intimacy we develop with a participant that is usually obscured in research findings. This makes it possible to also stand with participants on the page, and in the unfolding action, and goes some way to showing the philosophy underpinning our research.

Writing stories

When used as a methodology, stories provide one way of drawing together, presenting and making sense of – in an accessible and visceral account – field notes, interviews, action and events that a researcher witnesses in the course of her research. Such accounts can provide a mood and feel for how the data were collected, and invite dialogue such that the audience is not forced or channelled to accept a single finalised perspective (Clough, 2002; Frank, 2010).

Kitrina (first author) adopted such an approach to write: *My eyes got a little bit watery there* following fieldwork at the first Battle Back golf skills course in 2014, where she also carried out life-story interviews with two coaches, three members of the On Course Foundation team and seven military personnel on the course. Additional sources of ethnographic data were observation, field notes, a reflexive diary and discussion from sharing our research with the group and receiving feedback. Space limitations prohibit a full description of the methodological and ethical considerations of this approach, but these can be found in Douglas and Carless (2015b).

Saldaña (2011) provides an insight regarding how we approach writing stories:

> If you write with a message, moral or lesson in mind, the result is most often a heavy-handed, theme-driven fable rather than a character-inspired and story-driven drama. (p. 121)

Similarly, the story that follows is inspired by the lives of five characters and based on actual events, people and happenings. Our belief is that when we describe well the drama of life, that the emotional dimensions will be revealed in an authentic and contextual way that shed light on the questions we raise and our aims for this work. Namely, to understand the emotional demands of working among injured sick and wounded soldiers and to better support coaches in this area of disability sport coaching.

My eyes got a bit watery there

1. Packing

'Right love I'm off', Alwyn called up the stairs. Annie's head came into view over the bannister, smiling.

'And you're not taking these?' She held a pair of shoes in one hand and a wash-bag in the other.

'Oh heavens', he said coming up the stairs again. They met on the landing, where she threw her arms round his neck, still holding the shoes and wash bag, as he slipped his arms round her waist. There was a sense of security here, and normality, of deep respect, care, love, but it seldom came out in words. There was so much they didn't say, there was so much he couldn't seem to put into words.

It was like that the first time he'd come back from coaching injured soldiers. During the actual coaching, he felt he'd done a good enough job. It had been challenging all right, trying to find a way for a man with two prosthetic legs to make a backswing and keep his balance, and then helping another man with other complex injuries to find his rhythm. Oh, and the man who'd lost three fingers, and … it went on. He held himself together despite some of the stories the men had shared about their injuries. Then, at the end of the week, just before they all left, one of the men came up and just grabbed him, gave him the biggest hug he'd ever experienced. This huge burly soldier nearly squeezed the life out of Alwyn. Then he said something that left its mark. He said, 'Mate, you've changed my life, you've given me my competitiveness back, you've rekindled the fire'.

That experience, of being held and completely enveloped in another man's arms, brought a deeper level of understanding about what he'd been doing all week. He hadn't thought about rekindling a fire in someone's life. The enormity of *that* only took hold of him when he finally got home. Then, he sat down and just sobbed. Where did those emotions come from he wondered? How could he explain *that* to Annie? They'd been together for forty years. Bit-by-bit he shared snippets with her and of late, when he'd come back from coaching the war 'vets', Annie had got into the habit of pouring him a little whiskey, closing the door and slipping out to leave him alone for a moment or two in quiet contemplation. After half an hour or so, when he'd composed himself, let the emotions pass, he would find her and they'd begin to talk.

'These boys are so young', he would say to her. Coaching injured soldiers had now coloured life in a certain way, it changed him, humbled him and sometimes troubled him.

He broke off the hug.

'I need to get going, it's a new group called *Battle Back*, so I don't want to be late!'

Annie put the shoes and wash-bag into his waiting arms and kissed him once more, this time on the forehead. 'See you Friday', she said, and he was off.

***

There were six different piles on the bed. The first was a pile of socks, the second a pile of underpants, the third a pile of shirts and so on. Each pile was extremely neat, in-line and ready to pack. Peter had become aware that the more he was able to control his environment, the less he would be troubled by his anxiety. Going down a day early to Battle Back was absolutely perfect for him, as he couldn't cope with the unexpected, of being asked to do something without having time to think. His anxiety increased even as he thought about not knowing the times for meals, where his room would be, what would be expected of him and of interacting with other people. On a scale from zero-to-ten, the packing had raised his anxiety from zero-to-four, but at least he could take his time.

His mum popped her head round the door. 'What time you off pet?' Peter had been living with his mum since his divorce. His mum had, in many ways, always been a rock, a person he could depend upon, and at the same time she was the glue that helped hold him together. He didn't necessarily confide in her, but it was comforting knowing she was *there*, wherever *there* was.

As a boy, he'd been aware of a deep fear about becoming nothing, empty, black, devoid of love, touch. He was aware such thoughts might sound silly to others, so most times he didn't talk about them. But he could trace when it started. He remembered one night lying in bed when he was about six, and becoming consumed with the thought that, *you're not just dead for a million years, but for millions and millions of years*. Somewhere in his being, the meaning of this was like being caught by fingers of death and being dragged away. It was too much – he burst into tears and ran downstairs crying.

'What is it love?' his mother had asked, collecting him in her arms.

But he couldn't tell her. He couldn't give shape to the fear, to name what it was that troubled him. All he felt able to say was something quite different: 'I've a pain in my legs mum'. He remembered how his mother tried to soothe the pain away by stroking the palm of her hand down his shins, along his little bare feet, up over his calves all the while cradling him in her arms and gently rocking him back and forth with his head tucked under her chin. Did she know there was more? Could she tell there was something unspeakable troubling her little boy? And did she know now that her grown son was experiencing more profound panic attacks and acute anxiety, with physical manifestations, a fear that made his heart race, his stomach retch and his whole body tremor. Did she know it was triggered while he was serving his country, standing with his brothers in some desert miles from home?

He knew most times he could hide it, as his mum popped her head round the door, it was still four and he felt safe. He looked at his watch and responded to her question. 'I'm leaving now!' There was no more time to procrastinate.

2. *Fear*

'Right', said the tall, slim man rubbing his hands together and looking round the room. His voice was slightly louder than the upbeat background music, slightly louder than conversations and slightly louder than he would talk normally. Faces turned as he attempted to make eye contact with thirteen men and one woman seated round the periphery of the bright room, which at that moment was bathed in sunshine.

'My name is Greg, and I'm the course leader this week. This is the first time we've run a golf skills course, and I for one am looking forward to it'. He smiled while pointing a remote control towards the music to kill the sound. With that he sat down and lowered his voice. Greg was a keen golfer and had worked with several pro golfers over the years, helping them improve their mental skills and performance. That knowledge, he thought, would be useful now as he considered how to steer the morning session.

'I wonder', he asked leaning forward on his chair and looking at the faces before him, 'would it be alright if we begin by everyone introducing themselves?' His voice had become softer. 'And maybe, if you wouldn't mind telling us what you'd like to get out of the week? Or', he paused and smiled, "what would make it a really good week for you?'

***

Peter had been counting the number of people to his right in the circle; he knew there were three men left to speak before he would be expected to say *what would make this a great week*. It was like a shadow creeping towards him as he became increasingly more anxious. Walking into the room had set him off. Now he could feel his heart pounding in his chest, his hands becoming wet and his body hot. A knot of tension was growing, as were feelings of self-consciousness. He knew the beads of sweat forming on his forehead were visible. He was being sucked down into whirlpool of mud, soon to disappear like a shoe sucked beneath the surface. There was no escape.

Everyone else is answering, he told himself. *I have to*. Suddenly, it was his turn. Peter swallowed. 'I lost interest', he said, trying to speak slowly, to not show he was anxious. But he could hear *it* in his shaky voice. He continued trying not to stumble over his words. 'It would be good to see if I can get the bug back'. He hoped that would be enough, and it was. The man next to him took over. 'Bit like me, mate', Hugh smiled towards Peter. 'I haven't played golf for two years because of my injury'. Hugh then looked towards other members of the group, sharing his burden with them all. 'A big thing for me this week is to see if I still can play'. Peter felt relieved, a little safer – he'd done it. Speaking out, he realised, made him feel good, it gave him a little boost, his heart was still racing but the wave had passed, and he had floated. *Not bad for a man who won't go outta the house,* he thought.

3. Lessons

If, at the Battle Back centre, Alwyn had been out of his comfort zone, at the driving range he was in his front yard. 'Can I have your attention?' he called, drawing the group towards himself. 'In a minute I'm going to divide you into groups of three, and then you'll take it in turns to hit balls, and this is what I'd like you to try'. He mixed descriptions with demonstrations, attending to what he called *the basics:* how to hold the club, stand to the ball and take the club back. He wanted each person to practise three things and he told them he wanted to *polish* their skills. Then he sent them off to begin hitting balls while he started giving individual tuition.

What might have impressed you, but what you may have missed had you not been there, was how Alwyn, when asking about how an illness or injury might potentially impact swinging the club or playing golf, gently turned each soldier so that his back was facing the public area. That way, it was almost impossible for anyone to hear what was being said. Even so, Alwyn lowered his voice a little as he asked each man about what might be sensitive or difficult things to talk about. Then, as if allowing the information to be processed, he moved to the side and his speech raised in volume. He'd say something funny and encouraged each player with, 'That's right!' 'Well done!' 'You got it'.

As he worked with each individual he'd ask questions: 'How does that feel?' 'Is that hurting your leg?' 'Did that increase the pain?' 'Are you alright with that?' 'Can you try this?' 'Okay-lets, try this then'. Asking, gently encouraging, tailoring his advice and when it didn't go right, he'd just go, 'Oh, I am a clot', placing the blame for poor shots at his own feet, for not understanding each man's situation well enough.

***

'YES!' Owen called out, as another ball hit the fence at the end of the range. It was followed by another loud crack as his driver hit the next ball. Hugh, in the next bay, couldn't help being drawn in. 'Wish I could hit that far', he sighed to Peter as two synchronised heads turned to watch another ball disappear into the distance. When Owen's ball finally landed, he raised a hand as if to salute his supremacy and yelled,

'A-i-r t-i-m-e!'

Was it envy at the distance the ball travelled, or the way Owen's young body coiled up and released power that made Hugh dissatisfied with himself? It was hard to tell by just watching, which was what Jessie was doing. Before her were two men, poles apart in behaviour, one doing what had been asked by the coach, and doing it well, attending to the non-showy little things, the three little, unspectacular tasks. The other *not* doing what he was asked, he wasn't making progress *technically*, *consistently* or in any predetermined way. He was *just* hitting each ball as hard as he could, as far as he could and when they went well, he was loving it. But, he was influencing how the others in the next bay evaluated their skills, their shots, their swings.

Peter whispered to Hugh, 'Drive for show-putt for dough!'

'I know,' he replied, 'but I'd still like to hit it like that!'

'So would I,' confessed Peter, returning to his next shot.

Then Owen mishit a couple of shots sending the ball sideways. He didn't call anyone to look at those shots. Jessie noticed though. He caught her watching.

'What am I doing wrong?' he asked.

'You'll need to ask Alwyn,' was all Jessie would say. While she could have helped him, she also recognised that she wasn't there to coach. She was there as a researcher and didn't want to encroach. And anyway, Owen didn't appear to really want to improve his golf, or get better, she told herself, by way of excusing her action of *not helping*. He just wanted to belt the ball further than everyone else. Why waste her words?

4. Interview

'What will you do with my interview?' Peter responded after Jessie asked if she could interview him.

'Would you mind if I show you an example?' she replied.

'No, that's fine,' he said.

Jessie opened her laptop. 'This is a film from our mental health research, it's one man's story.' The laptop sprung to life, as did the seven-minute film. Peter felt awash in a sea of emotions watching the story unfold.

'See, if someone has never had a panic attack in their life,' he began as soon as the credits came up, 'they *say* they can understand what it's like, but I don't think they can.'

Jessie waited for him to pause and then asked, 'Do you mind if I record this?'

'No that's fine,' Peter continued, enjoying that what he was saying was important enough to record. 'If I get a panic attack I get tears streaming down my face, and I can be an emotional wreck' he continued.

Jessie listened, nodded, watched, then, because they'd been talking about Peter's weight gain earlier asked, 'Did you see the bodies of people in the film?'

'Yeah, I know, I know', Peter replied thinking back to the large, flabby runners in the film. 'It was quite, my eyes got a bit watery there watching it. Stuff like that I can relate to, it means a lot to me'. Peter realised that, since watching the film, he'd found it easier to open up and remember how he felt and why he didn't exercise more.

'See, being in the army, they can't see what's wrong, people kind-of look down their noses at you, so people with mental health stuff will keep it to themselves, and that's the worst thing you can do. You end up just bottling it up inside. What makes me worse is looking at myself in the mirror, and at what I used to look like. But if I can get that thinking through my mind,' he pointed at the laptop, 'like that man on there, it's never too late to do something, to get back into it.' Peter paused again. 'You see, when you have this anxiety and panic attacks it feels like your life is over.' Watching that video, it's given me a wee boost to get back running, 'cause if he can do it, I can do it. I like people to tell me I'm doing good at something. I like a bit of praise.'

5. Tuesday morning

Hugh took a drag of his 'rolli' and stubbed it out on the pillar directly outside the entrance. As he did, Greg walked past on his way to the morning session. 'Last one is it?' Greg asked, partly in jest, partly to allude to his dislike of smoking. He winked as he said it, without breaking stride. Hugh thought back to the previous evening when, over dinner, he'd been telling Greg about the past three years. 'My wife would say, *Do you fancy going on a picnic, or shall we go out for the day?* And I'd say, *No, I'm in too much pain.* But it was just an excuse. I was well enough but I just couldn't go, I just got more and more depressed'. By the time he'd finished talking, Hugh realised he was feeling more positive and had begun to make plans. He smiled and followed Greg inside.

***

'Not so hard!' Greg shouted. 'You want him to catch it!' Owen had thrown the ball so hard it had slipped through Peter's fingers. But, in a comical way, it had rebounded off his chest and found his waiting hands. 'Now I'm going to introduce a second ball, and then a third and a fourth, to see how many balls we can keep going between us at the same time. Here we go.'

'Al!' Greg shouted throwing the first ball to Alwyn who caught the ball and then threw it on to Owen, shouting his name. While that ball was going round, Greg introduced a second. 'Al,' he called again, throwing ball number two and, as soon as Alwyn had thrown the ball on to Owen, Greg threw him ball number three, then four, then five. What you would have seen, if you looked through the window, was a group working together, with no visible competition between them, no aggression, no hierarchy, no failures, lots of laughter and complete concentration. Each person part of a coordinated effort – memorising names, familiarity being created, sharing some*thing* and a sea of colourful balls criss-crossing in mid-air like the Red Arrows. What you wouldn't have been able to see were the seeds of joy and confidence growing. By the time the activity was over, Peter felt like his battery had been recharged.

'That was like drinking Red Bull!' he proclaimed.

'Just imagine if we started work like that every morning!' Hugh joked back.

Peter, in shock, realised he'd been standing in close proximity to other people, playing a game and really enjoying it. He hadn't experienced any signs of anxiety. He couldn't remember the last time he had *that* feeling. It was such fun he felt a huge sense of achievement welling up within. 'Where did that come from?' he asked Jessie as they sat down to talk during the coffee break.

***

It wasn't a Mexican wave, but you would have been forgiven for thinking it was. The only thing Henry, a former soldier and member of the on-course team, had asked was, 'How many of you are getting a medical discharge?' There they were, seated round the huge boardroom table at Fordingbrook Golf Club, waiting for sandwiches and their afternoon round of golf and, in the interim, having their *employment in golf* talk from Henry. Hugh raised his hand. Next to him, Owen raised his, followed by Peter. The show of hands continued round the table until every man on the course had raised his hand showing he was being discharged. Each hand signalled a life trajectory fractured by injury or illness and attested to an *end*. It was a sobering moment.

'My wife's boss has got some work for me, but I am still interested in what's available in golf,' Hugh offered.

'I want do accountancy,' Peter interjected. 'I wouldn't want to throw all that away to become a green keeper.'

'It's not just about green keeping!' Henry had been fiddling with a paper clip while listening. He stopped, opened his hands to the group and looked toward Peter before making eye contact with the others. 'There are over 600 different jobs you could go into in the golf industry. Agronomy, turf science, equipment design, engineering, course design and maintenance, marketing, managing golf clubs. We have loads of our guys working as club secretaries. Then there's logistics, communication. We've got contacts in every area of golf and we can open doors.' It was hard to disagree with a man with no legs.

6. Scoff

Harry Potter would be comfortable here! Alwyn thought, picking his way through the crowded dining room filled with gymnasts in brightly coloured Team GB tracksuits. There was only one empty place at the table between Peter and Owen, opposite a couple he didn't know. One of these men, Liam, was mid-way through telling a story. He broke off to nod, smile, make space and then it was back to the story.

'So, there I was with this Afghan woman sitting at the bottom of my bed ...' The others, Alwyn noticed, were transfixed. 'And then these girls turned up trying to sell me shit. I was shouting to the nurse, *Who the fuck are all these people in my room?* Those listening laughed. *Why are these people here? Get 'em all out so I can have some peace!*'

'I saw crabs crawling all over my body', the man next to him began, 'I was so out of it'. Alwyn had never taken morphine, or any of the other drugs they talked about for that matter. These guys seemed knowledgeable about all sorts of medications – the long names tripped off their tongues as they compared side effects. He was glad, sort of, to be included – even though some of the stories were hard to listen to. He couldn't help drifting off into his own imaginings, seeing the scene they were describing, what he might have felt like within it.

'All that effort draggin' him back', Liam's voice was now more sombre. The laughing had stopped. He'd begun another story. 'And I turned him over and he had no face, no legs – gone. And I hadn't even noticed. I dragged him all that way'. Alwyn was there, gripped, in that place, imagining a dismembered body before him, a lost friend, warm blood on his hands. He felt a tinge of sickness. Then he was back in the moment, sitting round the table, with little to say. The others, this time, were silent too.

Then Liam glanced at his watch and stood up and in a beautiful Irish lilt asked, 'You coming to the cinema?'

'Ah, no, you go ahead'. Alwyn returned to the present as the group around him gathered trays and empty plates, and departed.

Greg, seeing the vacant seats, shifted down the table. 'You guys do an amazing job', Alwyn offered. He'd never seen a group brought together like these coaches had done. He was amazed at the way Greg knitted together talks about behaviour, anger management, psychology, golf and life through little sport-stories and activities.

They began chatting at 20:08 and at 22:55, when Alwyn glanced at his watch again, he and Greg were still talking. Chewing the cud, some might say. Alwyn loved it. He'd never experienced this type of camaraderie between coaches and he was learning so much. It was so enriching to talk.

'I had a pro golfer come to me', Greg continued, 'he was just so down on himself. I asked, *Why don't you go yeaaaah! after a good shot?* That's like some of the guys here – they seem to have lost the ability to enjoy life, to enjoy the good shots, or get excited. Mind you, it's not surprising', he shrugged.

'I know what you mean', Alwyn paused, thought for a moment, then added, 'But, in golf, we have a saying', he drew closer as if to pass a secret, 'it's not how good your good shots are, it's how bad your bad shots are'. He sat back and smiled. 'So with the kids I work with, well, come to think about it even the Tour players, I try to get them to be more *even*'. As he said *even,* his hand mimed calming the troubled sea. 'You know, *not* excited on the good shots because they are only *part* of it. If they get excited they are focussing on the outcome. I kinda try and nurture the opposite, focus on the swing, the move, the feel. Does that seem like the opposite of what you are suggesting?'

Greg paused for a moment. Yes it did, but he could see merit in both approaches. 'I get that, I can see why you would do that', he nodded. 'But so many of these guys have become apathetic, indifferent, demotivated, beaten down. I feel we need to help them experience the fun in sport again, get 'em up a bit, encourage them like, even if its only for one shot or one moment at the range'.

'I'm with you there', Alwyn agreed. 'But if we're talking about playing golf longer term, the focus needs to be on the *process, the swing,* not the immediate outcome. So, as long as you focus 100% on making a particular move correctly, the shot outcome doesn't matter. It will, over time, get better. If it's just the outcome of the shot that matters, it will be a roller coaster ride. More importantly, the swing won't get grooved, you don't get the basics cemented. No?'

7. Wednesday morning

Hugh took a long drag of his 'rolli' and, as he did, Greg walk past. 'Last one is it?' Greg asked. A cheeky smile spread across his face as his eyebrows joined like paddles on a pinball machine: *ding ding*! Hugh laughed to himself, took one more drag, stubbed-out the 'rolli' and followed Greg into the morning session.

***

As the group began to arrive, one of the coaches popped a video on the TV hoping to bring some life to the quiet room. It was a mountain of a TV – you'd have a job *not* to watch it. And the video? Well, it was *blokes. Blokes* doing daring things, *blokes* throwing themselves off mountains, *blokes* throwing themselves out of aeroplanes, *blokes* throwing themselves from dangerous cliff edges. It was mad, wild, fast and mesmerised most of the group with colourful images and the fast beat of the music. Soon seats were filled and it was back to the flip chart.

'Morning', Greg greeted everyone. 'How are you all today?' He scanned the smiling faces. 'Quick session this morning then we're off to play golf.'

8. Silly bugger

You silly old bugger, a voice in Alwyn's head interrupted. *That's not the way you teach someone to swing a golf club!* Alwyn recognised the voice as his 20-year-old self – arrogant, proud, self-assured and over-confident. *Bloody impossible*! It had taken him thirty years to realise how simple he needed to make teaching the golf swing, and now, with younger coaches, he could hear the same attitude in their voices. They were all eager to use biomechanical analysis and the newest computer-aided technology on every player, just like he had been when he was twenty. *He needs to be in a much stronger position at the top of his swing*, the voice echoed again. *No! He doesn't you fool!* Alwyn answered. *He hasn't got the strength in his golfing muscles yet. OK, he might be able to carry 200 lb of ammunition and an injured mate and, yeah, he'd make short change of you if you got on the wrong side of him, but he can't hold that position at the top of his swing. He isn't a Tour pro!* Still, in his imagination, he shook his head. *You're constantly searching for this Aladdin's cave with the perfect swing in it*, he was now addressing all the arrogant young men who thought they knew how to teach golf, *and it's not there!*

He refocused, returning his thoughts to the man in front of him. 'You had a really good rhythm earlier, that's all you lost on that last shot. Don't try and change a thing, all that happened there was the sequence was out of synch'. Peter was listening intently and nodding. 'Did you try to hit the ball further?' Peter smiled. Alwyn took *the look* as a form of confession. 'Change the club if you need the ball to go further, not your swing', he smiled. 'I know, we all do it! Go back to thinking about your rhythm'.

Peter went to the side of the tee and took several slower, more rhythmical practice swings. Then he closed his eyes like Greg had shown him in the morning session. In his mind, he followed a simple practical skill to make him more aware of his thoughts and his body. He stood for a moment before opening his eyes and stepping onto the tee. Then he hit the most perfect tee-shot and beamed a huge smile.

'That's it!' Alwyn encouraged, just as chuffed as if he'd hit the shot himself.

9. *Thursday morning*

Hugh was an expert at rolling tobacco, even standing up, balancing the tin on the stub-it-out stand, he took only moments to fill, roll, lick and light. Then he took a drag and carried on the conversation with the others, releasing the smoke as he chatted.

'So, do you get preferential rates then?' he asked, amazed at the information he could pick-up from this informal group.

'Yeah, you want to ask at that club near you, or Henry will know'.

Greg walked past. 'Morning', he offered to the 'smoking' group, on his way to set up for the first session on the final day. 'Last one is it?' he called out as he disappeared through the opening door.

Hugh laughed, but no-one else got the joke. 'It's an *in* joke', he said, turning to look towards the entrance. At that moment Greg glanced back and two men momentarily held in each other's gaze. Hugh smiled and Greg nodded. His work was done.

Reflections on the story

Our aim with *My eyes got a bit watery there* was not to tell a story *about* specific emotions, but rather, much like assembling pieces of a jigsaw, to illuminate the importance of emotion within a particular coaching context. By adopting a storytelling methodology, we hope to have provided a way for others to walk with the characters and learn about their world; a world where a multiplicity of feelings, relationships, emotions and interactions are, at different times, both hidden and revealed. It is not our aim to discuss each issue raised – they are too numerous. Indeed, stories like this open up rather than close down possibilities for reflection (Frank, 2010). That said, we would like to comment on how the story fulfilled our aims of uncloaking some of the less-visible aspects of sport coaching.

Frank (2010), writing about why stories are important, suggests that the established view is to inform professional practice. Along such lines, *My eyes got a bit watery there* responds to calls for sport coaching research and pedagogy to be based on 'real world scenarios' (Jones & Turner, 2006; Morgan et al., 2012), represented in accessible language. Like Frank, however, we see a story like this as having additional ontological purchase. That is, a precondition for knowing how to act, is knowing what is expected of us in order to carry out a particular role. This relies on being able to define the self we want to become or claim (Nelson, 2001). To *become* a coach, and to become an excellent coach, a person will (or perhaps should) hold in mind a particular narrative structure. This structure, or template, is based on publically available narrative types that 'story' the actions required to fulfil the role, and provide assurance that they will be sanctioned and accepted by others within the culture. Our research in sport has suggested that this framework has become narrower than need be, and at times oppressively and damagingly so (Douglas & Carless, 2015b).

If, as Bredahl (2011) argues, coaching an individual with a disability requires a coach to *think differently* and develop greater levels of empathy and knowledge, then perhaps the more important function of the story presented is to influence (or challenge) narrow conceptions of a sport coach as some machine-like mainframe whose ability or skill is being able to convey highly complex technical information to achieve performance, health or educational outcomes. By making visible those aspects of coaching practice that are often absent and rendering them present – emotional openness, caring, the small, subtle easy to miss gestures that lead to relationships being built and developed, trust, empathic understanding – the story *validates* other ways of *being* a sport coach, expanding the repertoire to other coaches and means of coaching. To be more blunt, the story provides evidence to counter 'qualities' that often dominate in sport culture – being tough, strong, fast or hard – by providing concrete examples (back-stage and front-stage) of what counts in the process of claiming an identity as someone who cares. Because the story is dialogical, it allows these alternatives to coexist alongside examples of hegemonic masculinity and the performance narrative (e.g. the coach hiding his tears, a young soldier hiding his anxiety, the value placed on hitting the ball a long way).

When soldiers talk in our interviews about traumatic events such as injury, death or loss, we might ask them 'How did you deal with that?' The most common response has been, *Man up*. 'Man up', however, is what Nelson (2001) might describe as a 'narrative fragment' chiselled from the weightier hegemonic masculine story of how an individual should act when confronted with trauma, emotional distress or vulnerability. But this way of coping is not working for many soldiers, coaches, women or men (Etherington, 2000). Against this backdrop, the types of evidence we suggest is important to bring to light are the micro-relational components of relationship building where one small act (a word or gesture) follows another in what at first glance might appear a trivial series of behaviours. One example of this is the cigarette-break interactions between Hugh and Owen. In these exchanges, few words were said, no technical input occurred, it was 'only' an eyebrow being raised, a smile in passing, a quietly shared joke. Across the duration of the 5-day course, however, these 'little' actions were hugely meaningful and the weight of their meaning is carried in their emotional engagement. These types of story plot follow a relational narrative where *the other* is important, valued and worth listening to – not simply a person to be conquered.

Other evidence of this counter narrative, where sensitivity and empathic understanding can be seen, is Alwyn recognising a potentially embarrassing situation on the driving range. Avoiding what might be embarrassing for a student is, of course, important in all coaching but, given the experiences of this group where the rawness of injuries are still visibly on the surface of the body, sensitivity becomes even more important. The way Alwyn positions the soldiers sideways on the range, and lowers his voice so that others can't hear is an illustration of what makes his practice excellent. Yet this is the type of action that is difficult to instil in novice coaches – he isn't 'ticking a box' but enacting emotionally awareness and sensitivity. We might go so far as to say that perhaps, without the types of emotional responses that Alwyn had previously experienced (feeling what it was like being held in the vice-like grip of another man, hearing stories of death and injury) it may be difficult to understand the meaning and significance of his actions.

Alwyn is an excellent coach, but what makes him excellent is not his technical knowledge about the golf swing, even though this knowledge is a necessary element of his professional practice. Rather, what makes him excellent, as opposed to average, is his level of emotional presence, his availability to those he coaches. He doesn't block the possibility of sharing experiences or hearing stories, he is *with* them in an emotional, human fashion. Part of this process is for Alwyn to be open to himself, reflecting, considering and allowing his emotions (at times) to bring meaning and significance to events that he can only imagine. Sometimes, these thoughts and feelings bring him pain, discomfort and great sadness. He is a 'bystander' who wonders what we are doing sending young men to war. One of the costs, therefore, of being empathic, caring and open to others is the risk of being unable to make things right, unable to answer moral questions and even to potentially experience vicarious traumatisation (Etherington, 2000).

By bringing these issues to light, we hope the story will help novice or inexperienced coaches appreciate what 'works here'. It should also pre-warn those entering this type of context about some potential benefits and risks of becoming caring and empathic. And they do come with a cost: those of us who advocate for them should ensure we show this side of the story as well.

The need for stories in coaching research

Traditional approaches to research and representation (e.g. positivist/post-positivist studies presented as scientific or realist tales) often fail to be true to coaches' experience of what they do. *What* is reported and *how* it is reported often reflects the horizon of interest of academic researchers and scientists, preventing us from seeing what is before our eyes in day-to-day practice. Even when we do see, these ways of representing research can prevent coaches recognising their own practice in the literature, obscuring the best of what it is they actually *do*.

Alwyn's response after reading the story, although supportive and positive, wasn't lengthy. His action, however, revealed how he felt about it. He told us that he emailed the story directly to a close family member as evidence of his work. This action suggests the story 'spoke a language' that communicated something about his practice that he was proud of, but was less able to convey in words or through description himself. And isn't this often the case? While traditional research and representations about coaching practice may be true, they aren't true enough. In the process of content analysing and dissecting people's lives and experiences, meaning and connections are easily lost. One reason a picture speaks a thousand words is because it *shows* an image that is difficult to articulate. Likewise, the story *shows* something that people who have been part of the project recognise in a meaningful and emotionally connected way.

Military personnel on the course and staff involved in the project who read this story conveyed a belief that it carried, in a dynamic, true-to-experience way, important 'nuggets' that gave a *feel* for the essence of the programme. These responses suggested to us that *My eyes got a bit watery there* is more than just an accessible representation. Rather, the story makes it possible to touch on a truth as the individuals concerned experience it, within their own being and in a way that is not usually articulated or that they may not have previously been aware of.

In terms of coach education and pedagogy, if we wish to develop young coaches, we think the profession should aspire to reach this level of emotional engagement. We recognise that coaches are increasingly being put under pressure to 'produce results' and to conform to a singular narrative script of success. Our role, as educators and researchers, therefore, is to keep revealing and supporting 'different ways to be' a sport coach through counter narratives and alternative representations. Perhaps when 'man up' fails to be the dominant response to trauma, and we are able to hold and support each other, vulnerabilities and all, stories such as this one will lose their potency. Until then, we believe their impact provides some much-needed validation and insight.

Acknowledgements

The research on which this article is based was funded by The Royal British Legion as part of their commitment to helping the recovery of wounded, injured and sick servicemen and servicewomen. We would like to thank Lt Col. Ian Thomas, Kate Surman, David Sewell, and the participants we know as Alwyn, Owen, Hugh and Peter for their feedback on an earlier draft of this paper.

Disclosure statement

No potential conflict of interest was reported by the authors.

References

Anderson, E. (2005). *In the game*. Albany, NY: SUNY Press.

Antoine, K. (1996). The role of the coach in training an athlete with a disability. *British Journal of Therapy and Rehabilitation, 3*, 436–439.

Bredahl, A.-M. (2011). Coaching ethics and Paralympic sport. In A. R. Hardman, & C. Jones (Eds.), *The ethics of sport coaching* (pp. 134–146). London: Routledge.

Bruner, J. (1990). *Acts of meaning*. Cambridge, MA: Harvard University Press.

Carless, D. (2012). Negotiating sexuality and masculinity in school sport: An autoethnography. *Sport, Education and Society, 17*, 607–625.

Carless, D. (October, 2014). Narrative transformation among military personnel on an adventurous training and sport course. *Qualitative Health Research,* 24, 1440–1450.

Carless, D., Peacock, S., McKenna, J., & Cooke, C. (2013). Psychosocial outcomes of an inclusive adapted sport and adventurous training course for military personnel. *Disability and Rehabilitation, 35*, 2081–2088.

Carless, D., & Douglas, K. (2010). *Sport and physical activity for mental health*. Chichester: Wiley-Blackwell.

Côté, J., & Gilbert, W. (2009). An integrative definition of coaching effectiveness and expertise. *International Journal of Sports Sciences and Coaching, 4*, 307–323.

Clough, P. (2002). *Narratives and fictions in educational research*. Buckingham: Open University Press.

Dallos, R. (2006). *Attachment narrative therapy*. Berkshire: Open University Press.

DePauw, K. P. (1990). Teaching and coaching individuals with disabilities: Research findings and implications. *Physical Education Review, 13*, 12–16.

DePauw, K. P., & Gavron, S. J. (2005). *Disability and sport* (2nd ed.). Champaign, IL: Human Kinetics.

Douglas, K. (2009). Storying myself: Negotiating a relational identity in professional sport. *Qualitative Research in Sport, Exercise & Health, 1*, 176–190.

Douglas, K. (2012). Signals and signs. *Qualitative Inquiry, 18*, 525–532.

Douglas, K. (2014a). Challenging interpretive privilege in elite and professional sport: One [athlete's] story, revised, reshaped and reclaimed. *Qualitative Research in Sport, Exercise and Health., 6*, 220–243.

Douglas, K. (2014b). Going home. In T. Adams & J. Wyatt (Eds.), *Stories of presence and loss* (pp. 103–114). Rotterdam: Sense.

Douglas, K., & Carless, D. (2008). Using stories in coach education. *International Journal of Sports Science and Coaching, 3*, 33–49.

Douglas, K., & Carless, C. (2015a). Finding a counter story at an inclusive, adapted, sport and adventurous training course for injured, sick, and wounded soldiers: Drawn in-drawn out. *Qualitative Inquiry, 21*, 454–466.

Douglas, K., & Carless, D. (2015b). *Life story research in sport: A narrative approach to understanding the experiences of elite and professional athletes*. London: Routledge.

Etherington, K. (2000). Supervising counsellors who work with survivors of childhood sexual abuse. *Counselling Psychology Quarterly, 13*, 377–389.

Frank, A. W. (2004). *The renewal of generosity: Illness, medicine, and how to live*. Chicago, IL: University of Chicago Press.

Frank, A. W. (2010). *Letting stories breathe: A socio-narratology*. Chicago, IL: University of Chicago Press.

Hochschild, A. R. (1983/2003). *The managed heart*. Oakland, CA: University of California Press.

Jones, R., & Turner, P. (June, 2006) Teaching coaches to coach holistically: Can problem-based learning (PBL) help? *Physical Education and Sport Pedagogy, 11*, 181–202.

Jowett, S. (2005). On repairing and enhancing the coach–athlete relationship. In S. Jowett, & M. Jones (Eds.), *The psychology of coaching* (pp. 14–26). Sport and Exercise Psychology Division, Leicester: The British Psychological Society.

Lyle, J. (1999). Coaching philosophy and coaching behaviour. In N. Cross & J. Lyle (Eds.), *The coaching process: Principles and practice for sport* (pp. 25–46). Oxford: Butterworth-Heineman.

McLeod, J. (1997). *Narrative and psychotherapy*. London: Sage.

McGannon, K. (2012). Am "I" a work of art (?): Understanding exercise and the self through critical self-awareness and aesthetic self-stylization. *Athletic Insight, 14*, 79–95.

Midgley, M. (2001). *Science and poetry*. London: Routledge.

Morgan, K., Jones, R. L., Gilbourne, D., & Llewellyn, D. (2012). Changing the face of coach education: Using ethno-drama to depict lived realities. In P. Potrac., J. Denison, & W. Gilbert (Eds.), *Handbook of sports coaching* (pp. 520–533). London: Routledge.

Nelson, H. (2001). *Damaged identities, narrative repair*. Ithaca, NY: Cornell University Press.

Potrac, P., Jones, R., Purdy, L., Nelson, L., & Marshall, P. (2013). Toward an emotional understanding of coaching practice: A suggested research agenda. In P. Potrac, W. Gilbert, & J. Denison (Eds.), *The Routledge handbook of sports coaching* (pp. 235–246). London: Routledge.

Saldaña, J. (2011). *Ethnotheatre: research from page to stage*. Walnut Creek, CA: Left Coast Press.

Wang, Q. (2013). Structure and characteristics of effective coaching practice *The Coaching Psychologist, 9*, 7–17.

Emotions, identity, and power in video-based feedback sessions: tales from women's professional football

Simone Magill, Lee Nelson, Robyn Jones and Paul Potrac

ABSTRACT

While video-based feedback has become an increasingly salient feature of practice in high performance sport, it has received relatively little attention in the coaching literature. Data for this study were generated through a process of collaborative critical reflection and cyclical, in-depth interviews with elite female footballers. Using fictional narratives as a mode of representation, we highlight the emotional, embodied, and relational features of two athletes' experiences of video-based feedback. Burkitt's writings addressing (complex) emotions and social relations are used as the primary sense-making framework. Consequently, the analysis is grounded in the interconnections between sensate, corporeal experience, and the power relations and interdependencies in which high performance athletes are enmeshed.

Introduction

The use of various video and computer based technologies to analyse, support, and monitor athlete performance has become an increasingly pervasive feature of high performance sport (Jones, Marshall, & Denison, 2016; Mackenzie & Cushion, 2013; Taylor, Potrac, Nelson, Jones, & Groom, 2017). However, the popularity of their application has not been matched by a corresponding amount of scholarly inquiry into their use. As argued by others, the critical understanding of such technologies as coaching tools is at an embryonic stage of development (Groom, Cushion, & Nelson, 2011; Groom & Nelson, 2013a, 2013b). Indeed, much of the available literature investigating the pedagogical utilisation of computer and video-based technologies has focused on their potential to support the skill learning of athletes. This work has tended to adopt a (post) positivist orientation, focussing on objective accounts of "what works" (e.g. Bertram, Marteniuk, & Guadagnoli,

2007; Guadagnoli, Holcomb, & Davis, 2002; Moreno et al., 2016). While such inquiry has contributed to the advancements of evidence based "good practice" guidelines, a call for more critical inquiry into the lived experiences of those subject to them has also arisen (Groom & Nelson, 2013a, 2013b).

Foundational work in this area has sought to document how the application of computer and video-based technologies are inextricably grounded in dynamic contextual relations between coaches, athletes, and a range of significant others. For example, Booroff, Nelson, and Potrac (2016) and Groom et al.'s (2011) investigations highlighted how coaches' understandings of the socio-political demands of organisational life influenced their use of computer based technologies, while Williams and Manley (2016) and Jones et al. (2016) addressed concerns regarding the potentially harmful and "controlling" impacts of such technologies. Similarly, Taylor et al. (2017) depicted an athlete's fears and disquiets regarding the continual video-based monitoring of her performances in training and competition and, relatedly, the public evaluation of her decision-making and actions. The subsequent insights generated have challenged the often dominant and functionalistic discourses surrounding the use of technology in sport. This critique, however, has not been universal. Here, Collins, Carson, and Cruickshank (2015, p. 1088) claimed that such work has "raised the alarm prematurely, inappropriately and on somewhat shaky foundations". In asserting that the essence of coaching is about "decision-making", they alternatively argued that such technologies can significantly "alter" (read improve) that decision-making and subsequent practice.

In engaging with this debate, we believe greater attention should be given to exploring the inherently emotional, embodied, and relational features of athletes' pedagogical engagements with performance analysis technologies. While educational theorising has increasingly recognised that learners (and teachers) experience a wide range of emotions (e.g. joy, boredom, excitement, and vulnerability) and embodied sensations as they engage with information, activities, and feedback from others (e.g. Christie, Tett, Cree, Hounsell, & McCune, 2008; Värlander, 2008), there has been little consideration of these issues in the context of sports coaching. Such inquiry then, can contribute to an epistemology of coaching that reflects "the bodily being in the world [and] what it is to be human" (Burkitt, 2014, p. 172). In doing so, it gives primacy to how emotion, "feeling and thought … are intrinsic in any situation we encounter" (Burkitt, 2014, p. 101).

The intention of this paper is to stimulate critical reflection on athletes' meaning making in video-based feedback sessions. This is particularly in terms of how their embodied expressions and feelings are "bound up in power relations and interdependencies" as manifest through such technologies (Burkitt, 1999, p. 128). In adopting a relational perspective, the purpose is to break new ground in the theorising of sports coaching by highlighting how emotions matter to our understanding of "action, culture, and self" (Walby, Spencer, & Hunt, 2012, p. 4). Here, we conceptualise emotion as "the experience of social relations" which takes place at the interface of the self and social structure (Walby et al., 2012,

p. 4). However, rather than delimiting the academic gaze to a particular emotional state (i.e. guilt or anger or joy), the significance of the paper also lies in its focus on the overlapping nature of "emotions in action" (Walby et al., 2012, p. 4). This is particularly in terms of how "emotions that characterise interaction" can "move from negative to positive and back again in rapid succession" (Stets, 2010, p. 267). In doing so, the study holds potential to generate rich insights into the dynamic "emotion flows" that are a feature of individual and collective work place experience (Stets, 2010; Wharton, 2014).

In terms of structure, the paper is divided into four sections. Following this introduction, the academic benefits of creative fiction and narrative representation are outlined. The primary sense-making framework deployed is then introduced; Burkitt's (2014) theorising on complex emotions. The inclusion of theory reflects the belief that scholarly work should entail more than presenting (hopefully) interesting and engaging stories (Jones, 2009; Potrac, Jones, Gilbourne, & Nelson, 2013). Like Denison (2016, p. 9), we believe "the obvious presence of social theory in our narratives" is important to the production of analyses of social life that recognise its complex and embodied nature. The two narrative fictions, which chart Megan's and Abigail's (pseudonyms) respective experiences of video-based feedback sessions in top-level women's football, are then presented. The stories not only seek to illustrate the various and sometimes contradictory emotions (e.g. fear, anger, guilt, joy, and pride) each experienced, but also their efforts to navigate relations with others. The narratives are accompanied by a suggested theoretical reading. The emphasis here is on illuminating how their emotional and embodied experiences are "to do with social relations and interdependencies", rather than being solely biological constitutions (Burkitt, 1999, p. 127). Finally, the key arguments are summarised, advocating greater critical consideration of the entwinement of emotion, social relations, and the pedagogical utilisation of video and computer based technologies in high performance sport.

Collaborative inquiry and the use of multiple methods

The methodology utilised in this paper was inspired by, albeit not totally beholden to, Titchen's (2003) notion of "critical companionship". Specifically, we utilised a collaborative process that entailed the gathering, evaluating, and critiquing of self, other and peer practice for the purpose of knowledge creation (Jones & Ronglan, 2017). At the core of this exercise was the detailed consideration of lived experience and personal consciousness, as well as the theoretical interpretation of them. This mode of inquiry then, combined "the expressive, intuitive process of relationships and creativity" with rigorous "analysis, critique, and evaluation" (Vanlaere & Gastmans, 2007, p. 764). In the context of this paper, we not only focused on developing rich descriptions of athletic experience, but also of making analytical headway concerning the unavoidable interdependence of emotion, identity, and social relations in video-based feedback sessions.

Traditionally, the collection, analysis, and writing-up of data are considered three distinct and sequential phases in the production of a research paper (Tracy, 2012,2013). In this study, however, they were fused together to form a cyclical and iterative process of inquiry; one that combined data generation, narrative writing, and emic and etic sense making (Taylor, 2014; Tracy, 2012, 2013). The data, and the stories we subsequently produced from them, were generated through concerted and co-operative critical reflection and debate that lasted for a period of 6 months (Chang, Ngunjiri, & Hernandez., 2013; Jones & Ronglan, 2017; Titchen, 2003). This began with me, the lead author, sharing written accounts of practice based on attendance at video-based feedback sessions as a professional footballer. This material was further supplemented with interview data obtained from 10 female professional footballers. Here, semi-structured interviews were used to explore understandings of such ("coaching") practice within wider work relations, learned subcultural expectations, and the management of contextual interactions. These accounts formed the basis for collective discussion, debate and exploration, which primarily occurred in weekly face-to-face meetings and, to a lesser extent, via email. During our discussions, my co-authors, Lee and Paul frequently asked me to "tell us more" about my specific embodied emotional experiences (Chang et al., 2013, p. 28). They also asked questions relating to "when" and "why" a player might display or hide certain emotions in this social milieu. Such questioning informed the cyclical interrogation of both mine and the interviewed players' experiences.

Alongside the generation of data, we also sought to develop a theoretical reading of the issues combined in my personal narrative and the players' interview transcripts. On one level, this entailed an emic, or emergent, reading of the data. This cycle of analysis comprised three phases; data immersion and primary-cycle coding, hierarchical coding, and writing (Tracy, 2013). The initial phase was used to fully consider the richness of the gathered data and to establish tentative ideas about, and descriptions of, the social processes evidenced within them. Following this, the developed codes were grouped into a hierarchical umbrella that sought to make conceptual connections between them (Tracy, 2013); what Richards (2005) referred to as analytical coding. That is, the coding was grounded in the interpretation of, as well as reflection upon, meaning. This aspect was driven by the aims of the research project and associated research questions (Merriam, 2009). Once the data had been organised and coded into appropriate themes, the stories presented in this paper were generated. Reflecting our shared emic consideration of the data, these narratives were based upon three inter-related assertions; (a) the interconnection of emotion and a playing identity, (b) the regulation of emotional displays, and (c) the precarious nature of employment in women's professional football.

These themes, as well as the codes and meaning units contained within them, were also subject to a process of etic analysis. Here, analytical memos were used to develop preliminary links from the data to potential explanatory frameworks

(Tracy, 2012, 2013). Although a variety of theoretical perspectives from the sociology of emotion literature were discussed (e.g. Bolton, 2005; Stets & Turner, 2014; Zembylas, 2006), Burkitt's (1997, 1999, 2002, 2014) corpus of work was ultimately adopted as a sense-making lens. Importantly, the etic readings raised further questions that prompted additional cycles of data generation, both in terms of my personal narrative and follow-up interviews with the players. Engagement with Burkitt's ideas supported the development of the final narratives presented in this paper, as they led us to consider already documented experience in a more detailed and nuanced way. Such an iterative and recursive approach to inquiry not only allowed social experience to be considered in an intimate manner, but also helped produce a deeper level of analysis than may otherwise have been achieved (Chang et al., 2013; Tracy, 2012, 2013).

Fictional narratives were chosen as a mode of representation for a variety of reasons (Gearity, 2014). Principally, as has been outlined elsewhere (e.g. Beames & Pike, 2008; Potrac, Nelson, & O'Gorman, 2016; Rinehart, 1998; Sparkes, 2002), for their ability to (1) highlight specific features of human experience, (2) stimulate discussion about such experience, and (3) inform lines of future inquiry aimed at enhancing our understanding of them. Barone (1997) argued that, when deployed in this way, fictionalised narratives have a legitimate and important role to play in social science scholarship. While the events presented in this paper could be considered as a "sociology of witness" (Frank, 1995, p. 23), the happenings, interactions, and people contained with the stories presented are both fashioned and dramatised (Denzin, 2013; Potrac et al., 2016). Accordingly, the characters featured are composite creations, not based on any one person but amalgams of several that featured in our discussions of the data. The ultimate concern of the stories was the explication of meaning making and social process, as opposed to a "factually correct" re-telling of any experience (Jones, 2006, 2009).

For this paper, two separate but progressive stories are presented (Purdy, Potrac, & Jones, 2008). The first, "Anxiety, humiliation, and (concealed) anger", focuses on the interplay between Megan's emotions; her interactions with the Head Coach, and, relatedly, her efforts to manage emotional displays in situationally expedient ways. The story seeks to illustrate the connections between specific emotions (e.g. anxiety, fear, and anger), identity, embodied experience, and an interpretive understanding of local power relations; in this case, the asymmetrical relationship that existed between Megan and the Head Coach. The second story, "Frustration, (concealed) pride, and self-loathing", develops this theme. Specifically, we consider how Abigail's experiences of specific emotions were not only reflected in the interconnection between her playing identity and understanding of subcultural values, but also in her immediate reluctance to avoid being seen not to act in the "right way" (Fineman, 2008, p. 7). Indeed, this story begins to address the "policing" role that colleagues, as well as coaches and managers, can play over an athlete's display of emotion within video-based feedback sessions (Haman & Putnam, 2008).

Theoretical framework: complex emotions and social relations

As stated, the primary theoretical framework used to guide our interpretations was Burkitt's (1997, 1999, 2002, 2014) work on emotions and social relations. His thesis rejects the reductionist, heavily psychologised explanations as limiting understanding of emotion to cognitive predispositions and neuro-circuits (Burkitt, 2014; Holmes, 2015). Equally, however, Burkitt (1997, 1999, 2002, 2014) cautioned against restricting accounts of emotion to solely social and cultural factors, believing it similarly led to the production of incomplete and misleading accounts of human experience. He suggested that although emotions "are products of both the body and discourse", they "are reducible to neither" (Burkitt, 2002, p. 153).

Rather than considering emotions to be expressions of inner processes, Burkitt (1997, 1999, 2002, 2014) positioned them as modes of communication within social relationships and interdependencies; as complex, relational, and embodied phenomena. The complexity of emotions lay in their intricacy, which include interconnections with the various aspects of human experience; that is, "the bodily, the discursive or linguistic, and the biographical" (Burkitt, 2014, p. 15). In his text, *Emotions and social relations*, Burkitt (2014, p. 15) argued that such a perspective allows a better understanding of how "socially meaningful relationships register in our body-minds and are [subsequently] felt" in social circumstances. At the heart of his theorising lay the belief that "without the body-mind, we could not feel our situations and patterns of relationships, yet without the social meaning of these relations, our feelings and emotions would be random and meaningless" (Burkitt, 2014, p. 15).

Burkitt's (1997, 1999, 2002, 2014) writings share many similarities with the relational theorising of Emirbayer (1997), Gergen (2009), and Crossley (2011). Here, emotion is not regarded "as a thing or substance that exists separately from relationships", but is performed within our interactions with others and the world around us (Burkitt, 2014, p. 18). In illustrating the point that there would be no emotion "without that relational sense", Burkitt (2014, p. 15) argued that we cannot love or hate anyone without reference to the ways in which that individual is related to us within a social encounter or context (Burkitt, 2014). It is this relational component that gives our "feelings meaning and sense, in that when we love or hate someone it is usually for a reason to do with the way that they have affected us or the way they have behaved in a certain situation" (Burkitt, 2014, p. 15).

Burkitt's (2014) perspective also recognised how an individual's emotional experiences are connected to wider cultural norms and practices; for example, social class, ethnicity, and gender relations. The belief thus exists that networks of relations both intersect and overlap allowing no separation of "the macro- the relations between classes, groups, and factions- from the micro- the face to face interactions of particular situations" (Burkitt, 2014, pp. 20–21). However, while acknowledging that local contexts are influenced by wider networks of social relations, Burkitt (2014) argued that this does not happen in an overly-deterministic manner. Rather, he suggested that, although people may script emotional scenarios and encounters, they also bring with them emotional dispositions that have developed during the course of their respective biographies (Burkitt, 2014). As such, social relations retain elements of dynamism, unpredictability, and are ultimately co-created, with no one person in total control over their development (Burkitt, 2014). Burkitt (1997, 1999, 2002, 2014) also suggested that within social networks, varying degrees of power exist that have ramifications for both individual and collective emotional experience. For example, some individuals may have more influence than others, which can manifest itself in tensions, conflicts, jealousies, and rivalries.

Burkitt's (1997, 1999, 2002, 2014) perspective also acknowledged that emotions have corporeal and embodied aspects. In drawing upon the work of Bourdieu (1979/1984), Dewey (1922/1983), and Elias (1978) among others, Burkitt (1999, p. 36) described how people appropriate "certain forms of bodily carriage and movement", as well as "ways of handling objects and manipulating them, which are culture specific". Rather than simply suggesting that the body comes into situations with "ready-made feelings and muscular experiences", Burkitt (2014, p. 116) argued that "the body is also essential in making (rather than simply experiencing) meaning". In striking a note of caution, however, he also warned against understanding embodied experience biologically, as opposed to through language and social meaning. Instead, he contended:

> speech, like feeling, is one of the uses and modulations of our body … what we feel and think is never something different from the sense of speech and, more generally, of language and social meaning. (Burkitt, 2014, p. 15)

Megan' story: anxiety, humiliation, and (concealed) anger

It had been a great week. The sessions had been fast paced, the level of play high, and the banter sharp. I was also revelling in my status, as the younger players sought my advice. I was training well. I felt light, energised, happy. However, as the first game of the season drew closer, the tension on the training ground became palpable. There were more over-hit passes, the players' first touches were not as crisp and controlled. Accusing looks accompanied the breakdown of any pattern of play. I watched his face increasingly darken. *He's worried we're going to make him look bad! And kick-off is just 24 h away.* As we arrived back at the team hotel, he announced an evening meeting. My heart sank. It was the way he said it; the hard-edged speech, arms folded across his chest. *He has more to say.* My body reminded me of painful times gone by. My stomach churned. I was worried.

I arrived early for the meeting. Twenty-two seats were neatly organised into two rows in front of a large video screen. I took my place in the front row, where the senior players were expected to sit. As the others filed in, my anxiety increased. I couldn't help it. *Maybe it'll be ok? Maybe there's nothing to worry about.* The room was quiet. I fiddled with my phone. *I know most of us found these sessions uncomfortable.* My chest tightened. As he entered the room, I quickly switched off my phone and sat upright.

He began by emphasising the need for good habits, of striving for continuous improvement, and the need to repay the club's investment in us. Steve, the performance analyst, had loaded footage from a recent game. *Oh no, not that one! That was awful. Why is he showing that?* I shifted uncomfortably in my chair. Steve pressed play. *How is this supposed to motivate us for the game tomorrow? Why is he doing this? Keep looking him in the eye.*

The video played. The section was entitled "Missed chances". The first clip showed me bearing down on the opponent's goal. *Here we go.* I felt sick. I hit my shot cleanly but the goalkeeper made a good save. *I should have scored. I really should have done better. I know, I know.* Heat rose through my body. My face reddened. He paused for a second then replayed the clip in slow motion. *Noooo. Why?* My miss looked even worse. *This is so belittling.* He paused the footage. I locked my knees tightly together. "That was a great opportunity for us there. The quality of the first touch is important. A not so good one has made the angle for the shot even more acute". The pulsing heat in my cheeks intensified. He looked me in the eye. "I know a shot to the near post may surprise a goalkeeper, but I think we really need to aim for the far post in these situations. We won't get too many chances like that at this level, so we must make the most of them". He puffed out his cheeks. "Everyone ok with that?" *I know, I know.* As I nodded, my ribs squeezed. I could feel eyes boring into me from behind. I felt naked, on display. I wanted to tell him. *This isn't helping me at all! All it does is make me anxious. I scored 20 goals last season or have you forgotten?* Of course, I didn't. *Conformity is everything.* The last person to do that was gone; labelled as having a bad attitude. I sat straight backed. The team talk moved on. I tried hard to look at him and listen but couldn't focus anymore. The damage had been done. *Come on, Megan. This is just how it is. Accept it and move on. You can't afford not to.*

Making sense of Megan's story: a relational reading

In developing a theoretical interpretation of Megan's story, we used Burkitt's (2014, p. 86) contention that "there is no emotion without a reason". Our sense-making illustrates how Megan's emotions were inextricably linked to her identity as a professional footballer and her relations with others in this context (Burkitt, 2014). For example, Megan's anxiety reflected her previous experiences within the subculture of professional women's football more generally, and the identity threatening nature of this video feedback session more specifically (Burkitt, 2014). Such a paranoid outlook is in keeping with the work of Thompson, Potrac, and Jones (2015), which highlighted the "dark side of organisational life" (Hoyle, 1982, p. 87) in professional football as manifest in a neophyte coach's subjugation to ceremonial "degradation". Here, the coach's workplace identity "was [publicly] transferred into something lower in the local scheme of social types" by his more senior colleagues (Garfinkel, 1956, p. 420). This was what Megan feared for herself in the feedback session.

Similarly, the embarrassment and guilt Megan experienced when watching (and re-watching) the video clip reflected the salience of her identity as a professional footballer, the non-verification of this identity by the coach, and its playing out in front of her peers (Burkitt, 2014; Turner & Stets, 2005). Turner and Stets (2005) suggested that when an identity is high, the failure to have it confirmed by others can produce strong negative emotions, which include embarrassment, shame and guilt. Megan's guilt also reflected her belief she had failed to live up to subcultural expectations regarding appropriate role performance (Burkitt, 2014; Turner & Stets, 2005), while her anger was a defensive response to what she considered a shaming public evaluation from someone in authority (Turner & Stets, 2005).

Megan's experience of these emotions was clearly embodied. The blushing of her cheeks, for example, reflected her understanding of personal shortcomings being critically dissected in public. Similarly, her effort to control bodily deportment represented a desire to maintain poise in an identity challenging situation (Burkitt, 2014). Rather than being a solely cognitive phenomenon, Burkitt (2014) argued that the self is based on feeling, and ought to be understood as such. Indeed, Megan's understanding of her professional footballer self was a "deeply felt entity" that, when perceived to be threatened, included a variety of physical sensations which could not be separated from the intonations, words, and evaluations of others (Burkitt, 2014).

Despite experiencing visceral feelings of anger at her treatment, Megan suppressed their public expression. Her efforts illustrate Hochschild's (1983, 2000) notion of "surface acting". According to Hochschild (1983), surface acting occurs when an individual regulates his or her emotions to create a situationally appropriate and "publicly observable facial and bodily display" (p. 7). Here, the emphasis is on "deceiving others about how we are really feeling without deceiving ourselves" (Hochschild, 1983, p. 33). For Megan, this not only required the active management of various sensations, but also the maintenance of a bodily deportment that demonstrated her deference to, and respect for, authority (Burkitt, 2014). This was both stressful and alienating, and required considerable emotional stamina on her part (Burkitt, 2014; Hochschild, 1983).

Megan's surface acting arguably reflected two interconnected factors. The first was the role script she was expected to comply with as a professional footballer (Burkitt, 2014; Hochschild, 1983). Here, her socialisation experiences led to clear perceptions of the display and feeling rules that were situationally appropriate (Hochschild, 1983). For Hochschild (1983), display rules focus on "when" and "how" overt expressions of emotion should occur, while feeling rules refer to the specific emotions that an individual should experience in a situation. In turn, Burkitt (2014) highlighted how these rules are shaped by dominant power relations. That is, they should not be understood separately from other agents' efforts to use emotion to "direct the field of social action"; to control and manipulate others (Burkitt, 2014, p. 150). In this case, Megan not only considered her anger to contravene the feeling and display rules expected, but also recognised that its display could have significant ramifications given the asymmetrical power relations that existed (Jones et al., 2011). Hence, she considered the public expression of her anger to represent a deviant act, which could stigmatise her as having a "bad attitude" (Cushion & Jones, 2006). It was a label that could not only have a detrimental effect on her immediate selection in the team, but also her continued employment at the club. Megan's attempts to regulate her emotions, then, also reflected her understanding of the uncertain nature of her work. Here, she considered the regulation of her emotions an essential strategy for navigating the demands of "a competitive labour market ... characterised by a constant surplus of talent" (Roderick & Schumacker, 2016, p. 167; Thompson et al., 2015).

Abigail's story: a tale of (hidden) frustration, (concealed) pride, and self-loathing

We'd lost the game. I clasped my hands together in anticipation. *I did ok. More than ok in fact. I was "the player of the match". He'd told me. Those extra hours of training were paying off!* As the video highlights loaded onto the big screen, he asked the usual question, "What are your thoughts?" I raised my hand. Before I could speak, our captain interjects; "We weren't good enough, too many mistakes. All over the pitch, no one looked up for this game!" Another senior player piped up, "The intensity and desire just wasn't there. Everyone needs to look in the mirror". The coach nodded his head in agreement. My shoulders sagged. *I should know by now. This is what always happens.* I lower my hand. Nobody noticed. I closed my eyes. *That was lucky. What was I thinking there*? I put on my "we must do better face". I disagreed with most of what was said. I hated what they were doing. *That's right, blame the younger players. You know they won't say anything back. That's how you cover up your mistakes.* I dug my nails deep into my hands. I said nothing.

He asked for the first clip to be played. The "in-possession" title flashed across the screen. *It's me.* I'd received the ball in the middle of the pitch. Three defenders closed me down; I lost the ball. *Think Abigail. What could I have done better there*? My stomach rolled. My breathing accelerated. *I had no-one to pass to. I was isolated. I can't say that. I can't blame them.* "Abigail, what do you need in this situation?" *Think Abigail, quick.* "I should have held the ball up better and waited for the support to arrive". *That should do it.* "Well actually, you needed support to arrive much earlier" he replied. The tension released. "The initial position you took up is spot on, your first touch is great. I can't really ask more of you there" he continued. I had to work hard to stifle a smile. I made sure not to make eye contact with anyone. *I can't be seen to be happy. They'd have something to say.*

He turned to the group. "Midfielders, how could you have helped Abigail in this situation?" *This should be interesting.* "No-one wanted to get there. There's got to be more desire" said a senior voice from the back. "Some of the younger ones have to do things quicker. They're forcing me to play deeper than I ought to. I just can't get there" *Hang on, don't blame the kids! You're part of the problem here. Look at the video. Focus on what the images are showing!* I felt my anger rising. The following conversation, however, moved away from events on the screen to banal generalities of "wanting it more than them", of needing to be "hungry for it", and the "young guns" needing to "wise-up". *This is bullshit! He's letting them do it again. At least one of them should have got closer to me in that passage of play. He never really takes them on, not really.* My body tensed. I wanted to call them out. *You're cheats and bullies.* But I said nothing. Thoughts of self-loathing raced through my head. *Come on, Abigail. Say something! This isn't right. You know it isn't.* I said nothing. *Maybe next time.* I looked down at the floor. *I'm on the team sheet. That's what really matters.*

Making sense of Abigail's story: a relational reading

Abigail's story sheds further light on the multi-faceted nature of an athlete's emotional experiences in a video-based feedback session. It charts feelings of pride, anger, and guilt, which were simultaneously grounded in her (embodied) identity, her understanding of contextual social relations, as well as her immediate reading of situational power dynamics (Burkitt, 2014). The pride experienced reflected the salience of her playing identity, her commitment to it, and her understanding of this identity being confirmed by significant others (Burkitt, 2014; Turner & Stets, 2005). Equally, her anger stemmed from her belief that senior players were failing to fulfil their normative role expectations in this network of relations (Burkitt, 2014; Turner & Stets, 2005). Furthermore, by consciously not challenging what she saw as unjust interactions, Abigail considered herself complicit in sustaining their potentially damaging impact on others (Turner & Stets, 2005).

Like Megan, Abigail engaged in the active management of her emotions and their expression. Her attempts to actively suppress visible signs of personal satisfaction (e.g. stifling a smile) reflected her understanding of subcultural expectations about appropriate feeling and display rules following a defeat, as well as her status within the relational system (Burkitt, 2014). To appear visibly happy with her own performance was, from Abigail's perspective, tantamount to transgressing widely held values related to the importance of collective responsibility for competitive outcomes. She thus understood that the failure to conform to subcultural norms could result in her being labelled as "selfish", "not a team player", and (like Megan) as having a "bad attitude". She feared marginalisation from the group (Burkitt, 2014; Haman & Putnam, 2008). It could be argued that Abigail's biography oriented her to make sense of this situation in a particular way, with "the patterns of her relationships from the past" being embodied in her understanding of the situation, her bodily dispositions, and her perception of others (Burkitt, 2014, p. 5).

Equally, the feelings Abigail experienced when deciding to publicly acknowledge, or suppress, her happiness at her performance reflected the contradictions, dilemmas, and paradox that are an inherent feature of organisational life (Burkitt, 2014; Jones & Wallace, 2005; Stacey, 2011). Here, Abigail experienced "a conflict of impulses", whereby she debated "two contradictory feelings … or impulses … in dialogical, polyphonic consciousness" (Burkitt, 2014, p. 135). Despite experiencing a clash of relational loyalties (i.e. to voice or suppress her views on the positive features of the team's performance), her understanding of situational demands featured significantly in influencing how she dealt with this emotional dilemma (Burkitt, 2014); that is, a strategy of silence and the outward expression of disappointment.

A particularly salient feature of Abigail's story was the importance attached to her peers' evaluations within the session. While their analysis of the team's shortcomings and apparent privileged status was a source of considerable anger for Abigail, she purposefully chose not to exhibit her irritation. Indeed, she felt powerless to address their behaviour in any meaningful way. Her outlook in this situation reflects Burkitt's (2014, p. 150) contention that "emotion is always interwoven in power relations, both shaping and being shaped by them". Here, Burkitt (2014) suggested that, as there are varying degrees of power within a social network, members' relationships with each other are rarely completely harmonious. Instead, he argued that the dynamics of power and status can lead to the formation of rivalries, tensions, and conflicts. In a similar vein, Walby and Spencer (2012, p. 186) claimed that there is much to be learned from exploring how "people narrate their frustration, indignation, and resentment" of formal and informal hierarchies.

Abigail's story also illustrates how emotion management in sport extends beyond the athlete-coach dyad to include a wider network of social actors (Burkitt, 2014; Crossley, 2011; Haman & Putnam, 2008; Nelson et al., 2013). While the academic literature has principally explored the emotional labour that occurs because of managerial surveillance and control, there has been a paucity of inquiry addressing how employees' expressions of emotion might be "controlled by other workers" (Haman & Putnam, 2008, p. 62). An exception was that by Haman and Putnam (2008) who highlighted how, to avoid conflict, individuals suppressed emotions in order to aid effective problem solving and the maintenance of co-worker relationships. They also avoided taking concerns to managers, as a "good employee" was considered not to make complaints about other staff members. Such social practices, Haman and Putnam (2008, p. 68) argued, can not only "become a source of great frustration and stress" but also "cause resentment to fester, lower job satisfaction, … and [could] lead to employee burnout".

Conclusion

The aim of this paper was to stimulate reflection on how high performance athletes' participation in video-based feedback sessions can be understood as emotional, embodied, and relational affairs. Building on previous work, as opposed to being critical of an uncaring or manipulative coach, the broad purpose was to tell of a "culture through characters"; of characters that engage, that feel pain and joy as they move through any given plot (Gilbourne, Jones, & Jordan, 2014). The value of the paper can be understood to exist at several levels. These include highlighting the various emotions (e.g. pride, guilt, anger) athletes experience in these pedagogically intended encounters, in addition to how these emotions are embedded in contextual "power relations and interdependencies" (Burkitt, 1999, p. 128). Indeed, Megan and Abigail's respective sentiments and feelings not only consisted of "sensate, corporeal components ... necessary to the lived experience", but were also socially constructed in nature (Burkitt, 1999, p. 116). That is, relations, behaviours, and feelings were inextricably intertwined (Burkitt, 1999, 2014). Here, emotions were grounded in Megan and Abigail's understandings of three inter-related factors: (a) the perception of their identity as professional footballers, inclusive of the reactions and evaluations of significant others; (b) their biographically informed beliefs about the precarious nature of their employment; and, (c) their understanding of dominant subcultural discourses regarding appropriate emotional dispositions (Burkitt, 1999, 2014). Importantly, the paper draws attention to how athletes' sense making of feedback sessions are always grounded in their understandings of the working culture and their place within it.

A further point we wish to raise here concerns the levels (or layers) of emotion management that athletes may engage in. Indeed, while Abigail's and Megan's stories explored emotion management in relation to separate coach-athlete and athlete-athlete relationships, an athlete may engage in these layers (and others) of emotion management simultaneously, thus adding another level of complexity to the phenomenon (Haman & Putnam, 2008). Consequently, while not a specific aim of the paper, the exploration of individuals' emotional management within a network of social relations represents a further potentially fruitful avenue for future inquiry if we are to understand better athletes' emotionality within high performance sport (Nelson et al., 2013).

Given the arguments made, we encourage coaching scholars to further examine the social relations in which coaching technologies are deployed and responded to by coaches and athletes (Mason, Button, Lankshear, Coates, & Sharrock, 2002). Such inquiry has the potential to develop accounts of the ways in which the pedagogical application of video-based feedback technology in particular, as well as coaching technologies more generally, cannot be known separately from the relations of power, interdependence, and communication in which social actors are enmeshed (Burkitt, 1999, 2014). A greater understanding of the intended and unforeseen consequences of using this technology could contribute to the development of a more finessed approach to its application; one where greater attention is paid to the social environment in which it is utilised, and the social sensibilities that underpin its application (Cameron & Webster, 2005; Taylor et al., 2017).

Finally, from a practical perspective, we recognise that video-based feedback is not of itself entirely unproblematic or, indeed, problematic (Collins et al., 2015; Taylor et al., 2017; Williams & Manley, 2016). As such, the question should not be to utilise video-based feedback sessions or not. Instead, it should focus on the intentionality of these sessions in relation to their possible latent effects. Here, coaches would benefit from reflecting upon how they frame and subsequently engage in these interactions; especially in terms of athletes' interpretations of them (Collins et al., 2015; Jones, Glintmeyer, & McKenzie, 2005). What is advocated here then is a call for coaches and coach educators to develop a historicising and scrutinising imperative of the wider structures within which elite sports performance occurs.

Disclosure statement

No potential conflict of interest was reported by the authors.

References

Barone, T. E. (1997). Among the chosen: A collaborative educational (auto) biography. *Qualitative Inquiry, 3*, 222–236.

Beames, S., & Pike, E. (2008). Goffman goes rock climbing: Using creative fiction to explore the presentation of self in outdoor education. *Australian Journal of Outdoor Education, 12*, 3–11.

Bertram, C., Marteniuk, R., & Guadagnoli, M. (2007). On the use and misuse of video analysis. *International Journal of Sports Science & Coaching, 2*, 37–46.

Bolton, S. (2005). *Emotion management in the workplace*. London: Palgrave.

Booroff, M., Nelson, L., & Potrac, P. (2016). A coach's political use of video-based feedback: A case study in elite-level academy soccer. *Journal of Sport Sciences, 34*, 116–124.

Bourdieu, P. (1979/1984). *Distinction: A social critique of the judgement of taste*. London: Routledge.

Burkitt, I. (1997). Social relationships and emotions. *Sociology, 31*, 37–55.

Burkitt, I. (1999). *Bodies of thought: Embodiment, identity and modernity*. London: Sage.

Burkitt, I. (2002). Complex emotions: Relations, feelings and images in emotional experience. *The Sociological Review, 50*, 151–167.

Burkitt, I. (2014). *Emotions and social relations*. London: Sage.

Cameron, A., & Webster, J. (2005). Unintended consequences of emerging communication technologies: Instant messaging in the workplace. *Computers in Human Behaviour, 21*, 85–103.

Chang, H., Ngunjiri, F., & Hernandez, K. (2013). Collaborative autoethnography. London: Routledge.

Christie, H., Tett, L., Cree, V., Hounsell, J., & McCune, V. (2008). A real rollercoaster of confidence and emotions: Learning to be a university student. *Studies in Higher Education, 33*, 567–581.

Collins, D., Carson, H., & Cruickshank, A. (2015). Blaming Bill Gates AGAIN! Misuse, overuse and misunderstanding of performance data in sport. *Sport, Education and Society, 20*, 1088–1099.

Crossley, N. (2011). *Towards relational sociology*. London: Routledge.

Cushion, C., & Jones, R. L. (2006). Power, discourse, and symbolic violence in professional youth soccer: The case of Albion Football Club. *Sociology of Sport Journal, 23*, 142–161.

Denison, J. (2016). Social theory and narrative research: A point of view. *Sport, Education and Society, 21*, 7–10.

Denzin, N. K. (2013). *Interpretive autoethnography*. London: Sage.

Dewey, J. (1922/1983). *Human nature and conduct: The middle works of John Dewey*. Carbondale, IL: Southern Illinois University Press.

Elias, N. (1978). On transformations of aggressiveness. *Theory and Society, 5*, 229–242.

Emirbayer, M. (1997). Manifesto for a relational sociology. *American Journal of Sociology, 103*, 281–317.

Fineman, S. (2008). *The emotional organization: Passions and power*. Malden, MA: Blackwell Publishing.

Frank, A. (1995). *The wounded storyteller: Body, illness, and ethics*. Chicago, IL: University of Chicago Press.

Garfinkel, H. (1956). Conditions of successful degradation ceremonies. *American Journal of Sociology, 61*, 420–424.

Gearity, B. (2014). Autoethnogrpahy. In L. Nelson, R. Groom, & P. Potrac (Eds.), *Research methods in sports coaching* (pp. 205–217). London: Routledge.

Gergen, K. J. (2009). *Realities and relationships: Soundings in social construction*. Cambridge, MA: Harvard University Press.

Gilbourne, D., Jones, R., & Jordan, S. (2014). Applied utility and the autoethnographic short story: Persusasions for, and illustrations of, writing critical social science. *Sport, Education and Society, 19*(1), 80–92.

Groom, R., Cushion, C., & Nelson, L. (2011). The delivery of video-based performance analysis by England youth soccer coaches: Towards a grounded theory. *Journal of Applied Sport Psychology, 23*, 16–32.

Groom, R., & Nelson, L. (2013a). The application of video-based performance analysis in the coaching process: The coach supporting athlete learning. In P. Potrac, W. Gilbert, & J. Denison (Eds.), *The Routledge handbook of sports coaching* (pp. 96–107). London: Routledge.

Groom, R., & Nelson, L. (2013b). The analysis of athletic performance: Some practical and philosophical considerations. *Sport, Education and Society, 17*, 687–701.

Guadagnoli, M., Holcomb, W., & Davis, M. (2002). The efficacy of video feedback for learning the golf swing. *Journal of Sports Sciences, 20*, 615–622.

Haman, M., & Putnam, M. (2008). In the gym: Peer pressure and emotional management among co-workers. In S. Fineman (Ed.), *The emotional organization: Passions and power* (pp. 61–73). Malden, MA: Blackwell Publishing.

Hochschild, A. (1983). *The managed heart: Commercialisation of human feeling*. Los Angeles: University of California Press.

Hochschild, A. (2000). *The time bind: When work becomes home and home becomes work*. New York, NY: Owl Books.

Holmes, M. (2015). Emotions and social relations. *Information, Communication and Society, 18*, 1430–1433.

Hoyle, E. (1982). Micropolitics of educational organisations. *Educational Management and Administration, 10*(2), 87–98.

Jones, L., Marshall, P., & Denison, J. (2016). Health and well-being implications surrounding the use of wearable GPS devices in professional rugby league: A Foucauldian disciplinary analysis of the normalised use of a common surveillance aid. *Performance Enhancement & Health, 5*, 38–46.

Jones, R., Potrac, P., Cushion, C., & Ronglan, L. T. (2011). *The sociology of sports coaching*. London: Routledge.

Jones, R. L. (2006). Dilemmas, maintaining 'face' and paranoia: An average coaching life. *Qualitative Inquiry. 12*(5), 1012–1021.

Jones, R. L. (2009). Coach as caring ('the smiling gallery'): Accessing hidden knowledge. *Physical Education and Sport Pedagogy, 14*, 377–390.

Jones, R. L. & Wallace, M. (2005). Another bad day at the training ground: Coping with ambiguity in the coaching context. *Sport, Education and Society, 10*(1), 119–134.

Jones, R. L., Glintmeyer, N., & McKenzie, A. (2005). Slim bodies, eating disorders and the coach-athlete relationship. *International Review for the Sociology of Sport, 40*, 377–391.

Jones, R. L., & Ronglan, L. T. (2017). What do coaches orchestrate? Unravelling the 'quiddity' of practice. *Sport, Education and Society, 1-11*. doi:10.1080/13573322.2017.1282451

Mackenzie, R., & Cushion, C. (2013). Performance analysis in football: A critical review and implications for future research. *Journal of Sports Sciences, 31*, 639–676.

Mason, D., Button, G., Lankshear, G., Coates, S., & Sharrock, W. (2002). On the poverty of apriorism: Technology, surveillance in the workplace and employee response. *Information, Communication and Society, 5*, 555–572.

Merriam, S. B. (2009). *Qualitative Research: A Guide to Design and Implementation*. San Francisco: John Wiley and Sons.

Moreno, M., Moreno, A., García-González, L., Ureña, A., Hernández, C., & Del Villar, F. (2016). An intervention based on video feedback and questioning to improve tactical knowledge in expert female volleyball players. *Perceptual and Motor Skills, 122*, 911–932.

Nelson, L., Groom, R., & Potrac, P. (2014). *Research methods in sports coaching*. London: Routledge.

Nelson, L., Potrac, P., & Groom, R. (2014). Receiving video-based feedback in elite ice-hockey: A player's perspective. *Sport, Education and Society, 19*, 19–40.

Nelson, L., Potrac, P., Gilbourne, D., Allanson, A., Gale, L., & Marshall, P. (2013). Thinking, Feeling, Acting: The Case of a Semi-Professional Soccer Coach. *Sociology of Sport Journal, 30*, 467–486.

Potrac, P., Jones, R. L., Gilbourne, D., & Nelson, L. (2013). Handshakes, BBQs, and bullets: Self-interest, shame and regret in football coaching. *Sports Coaching Review, 1*, 79–92.

Potrac, P., Nelson, L., & O'Gorman, J. (2016). Exploring the everyday realities of grass-roots football coaching: Towards a relational perspective. *Soccer and Society, 17*, 910–925.

Purdy, L., Potrac, P., & Jones, R. (2008). Power, consent and resistance: An autoethnography of competitive rowing. *Sport, Education and Society, 13*, 15–25.

Richards, K. (2005). Introduction. In K. Richards & P. Seedhouse (Eds.), *Applying conversation analysis* (pp. 1–15). New York, NY: Palgrave Macmillian.

Rinehart, R. (1998). Fictional methods in ethnography: Believability, specks of glass, and Chekhov. *Qualitative Inquiry, 4*, 200–224.

Roderick, M., & Schumacker, J. (2016). The whole week comes down to the team sheet: A footballer's view of insecure work. *Work, Employment and Society, 30*, 166–174.

Sparkes, A. (2002). *Telling tales in sport and physical activity: A qualitative journey*. Champaign, IL: Human Kinetics Press.

Stacey, R. D. (2011). *Strategic management and organisational dynamics: The challenge of complexity*. London: Prentice Hall.

Stets, J. (2010). Future directions in the sociology of emotions. *Emotion Review, 2*, 265–268.

Stets, J., & Turner, J. (2014). *Handbook of the sociology of emotions* (Vol. II, pp. 335–359). Dordrecht: Springer Science and Business Media.

Taylor, W. G. (2014). Qualitative Data. In L. Nelson, R. Groom, & P. Potrac (Eds.), *Research methods in sports coaching* (pp. 181–189). London: Routledge.

Taylor, W., Potrac, P., Nelson, L., Jones, L., & Groom, R. (2017). An elite hockey player's experiences of video-based coaching: A post-structuralist reading. *International Review for the Sociology of Sport, 52*, 115–125.

Thompson, A., Potrac, P., & Jones, R. (2015). I found out the hard way: Micro-political workings in professional football. *Sport, Education and Society, 20*, 976–994.

Titchen, A. (2003). Critical companionship: Part 1. *Nursing Standard, 18*, 33–40.

Tracy, S. (2012). The toxic and mythical combination of deductive writing logic for inductive qualitative research. *Qualitative Communication Research, 1*, 109–141.

Tracy, S. (2013). *Qualitative research methods*. Chichester: Wiley.

Turner, J., & Stets, J. (2005). *The sociology of emotions*. Cambridge: Cambridge University Press.

Vanlaere, L., & Gastmans, C. (2007). Ethics in nursing education: Learning to reflect on care practices. *Nursing Ethics, 14*, 758–766.

Värlander, S. (2008). The role of students' emotions in formal feedback situations. *Teaching in Higher Education, 13*, 145–156.

Walby, K., & Spencer, D. (2012). How emotions matter: Objects, organisations, and the emotional climate of a mass spectrometry laboratory. In D. Spencer, K. Walby, & A. Hunt (Eds.), *Emotions matter: A relational approach to emotions* (pp. 181–200). Toronto: University of Toronto Press.

Walby, K., Spencer, D., & Hunt, A. (2012). Introduction. In D. Spencer, K. Walby, & A. Hunt (Eds.), *Emotions matter: A relational approach to emotions* (pp. 3–8). Toronto: University of Toronto Press.

Wharton, A. (2014). Work and emotions. In J. Stets & J. Tuner (Eds.), *Handbook of the sociology of emotions* (Vol. II, pp. 335–359). Dordrecht: Springer Science and Business Media.

Williams, S., & Manley, A. (2016). Elite coaching and the technocratic engineer: Thanking the boys at Microsoft!. *Sport, Education and Society, 21*, 828–850.

Zembylas, M. (2006). *Teaching with emotion: A postmodern enactment*. Charlotte, NC: Information Age Publishing.

Index

For Product Safety Concerns and Information please contact our EU representative GPSR@taylorandfrancis.com
Taylor & Francis Verlag GmbH, Kaufingerstraße 24, 80331 München, Germany

www.ingramcontent.com/pod-product-compliance
Ingram Content Group UK Ltd.
Pitfield, Milton Keynes, MK11 3LW, UK
UKHW050753180926
475701UK00007B/1029

* 9 7 8 0 3 6 7 5 3 5 5 8 2 *